Fairey Rotodyne

Fairey Rotodyne

DAVID GIBBINGS

The History Press

First published 2009

The History Press
The Mill, Brimscombe Port
Stroud, Gloucestershire, GL5 2QG
www.thehistorypress.co.uk

British Library Cataloguing in Publication Data.
A catalogue record for this book is available from the British Library.

ISBN 978 0 7524 4916 6

Typesetting and origination by The History Press
Printed in Great Britain

Contents

Foreword

Most people remember their first flight in a helicopter. I certainly do – no clockwork mouse of a helicopter for me. My first flight in a rotorcraft was in the Fairey Rotodyne, and even after a lifetime spent flight-testing helicopters and aeroplanes, it still remains one of the most adventurous and exciting of all those various aircraft with which I became involved.

This book has grown from a lecture request from the Society of Flight Test Engineers, which was delivered in Berlin in 1994, and subsequently enlarged, to be offered as the forty-fourth Cierva Lecture, presented to the Royal Aeronautical Society in London, in 2003, the year in which we celebrated '100 Years of Powered Flight'. Now we have just marked '100 Years of Aviation in Britain', and the Rotodyne, having played a significant part in both events, deserves its place in history.

In 2007, I was asked to repeat the lecture as part of a celebration commemorating the first flight of the Rotodyne, in 1957, and it occurred to me that nobody has produced a book about this exciting aircraft in the intervening fifty years.

Here I will confess that I am very self-conscious of the fact that my personal involvement in the programme was as a very junior member of the team, joining towards the end. I have, however, been well placed in having access to what archive material is still available at Yeovil, and it is my hope that those who played a greater part in making this history will forgive my audacity.

As with all such books, there are a great number of individuals and organisations who deserve my thanks. Of these, I feel I must start with AgustaWestland, which is the current identity of my erstwhile employer, Westland Helicopters, and of the earlier Fairey Aviation. It is from this group that I was able to acquire the data, drawings and photographs necessary to compile this record, and the freely given permission to publish that has made it all possible.

My use of the Fairey logo on the cover gave me a surprise. I found it hard to establish who has ownership of this design, and my investigations led me to the General Dynamics Corporation, who may have inherited it through their involvement in Fairey Hydraulics. I was given the permission I required, although GD remains uncertain of the precise ownership. For myself, I thank them and trust that anyone else who may lay claim will appreciate that my request, which was made out of courtesy, also applies to them.

Flight International was, indeed, generous in granting permission to use their cutaway drawing, photographs and the article by Ron Gellatly, without any reservations. My negotiations with Andrew Costerton left me with a warm feeling that I was dealing with friends. It was no less the case when I sought permission to use material from *Aeroplane*; Michael Oakey was generous and accommodating, and both these great journals have my sincere admiration.

Producing art work to the high standards set by The History Press would have been considerably harder without the assistance of Doug Lloyd, who patiently accepted all my demands in spite of his own punishing work schedule. Doug is also responsible for the striking cover design; I know that you should not judge a book by its cover, but I can only hope that the content fulfils the promise implied by Doug's work.

The AgustaWestland photographic group deserve a special mention for the way in which they dealt with the numerous old negatives I presented them with. It is due to their efforts that there are several photographs, hitherto unpublished, that can now be seen in this book.

The Carter Aircraft Corporation and Groen Brothers Aviation of America are two companies who have picked up the challenge, and are currently working on projects that incorporate some of the technology that distinguished the Rotodyne. Both groups were extremely helpful, and I wish them the success that was so carelessly abandoned by faint-hearted officialdom so long ago. Remember: 'Fortune favours the brave!'

I have carefully avoided naming individuals within the book, on the grounds that the success of any venture relies upon the collective effort of all concerned.

For my own venture in the form of this book, I must acknowledge the help and support of friends and colleagues, many of whom are unaware that they have done anything: Fred Ballam, David Balmford, Tony Bamford, Mike Breward, Peter Bunniss, Bruce Charnov, Andrew Costerton, Pat Douneen, John Elver, John Fairey, John Firmin, David Groen, Mike Hirschberg, Dr G.S. Hislop, Anita Infante, Derek James, Alan Jeffrey, Doug Lloyd, Michael Oakey, Tony Pike, Norman Parker, Simon Prior, Ted Roadnight, Vic Rogers, Geoff Russell, Jim Schofield and John White. I am sure there are others, who have my apologies, but then, I am of an age now that I can claim 'a senior moment', so I am sure they will forgive me.

I feel that I must pay tribute to the memory of *Dipl Ing* August Stepan, for whom I worked during my time with Rotodyne. Working for 'Steppie' gave me a link with the past (he flew the Doblhoff jet helicopter on its first flight in 1944), and what I learned from him and his team steered the rest of my career in aviation.

The Rotodyne story is a tale of vision, ingenuity, achievement, unfulfilled promise and lost opportunity. What was achieved has stood the test of time; what was carelessly lost has given us cause to regret, and to wonder, it couldn't happen again, could it?

Definitions

HELICOPTER

A rotorcraft, which throughout its flight derives substantially the whole of its lift, control and translational thrust from a power-driven rotor system, whose axis (axes) is (are) fixed and approximately perpendicular to the longitudinal axis of the rotorcraft.

GYROPLANE (Autogiro)

A rotorcraft which, throughout its flight, derives the whole, or a substantial part, of its lift from a freely rotating rotor. The gyroplane provides propulsive power through its propeller, pushing or pulling (configuration dependent) the rotor through the air to sustain level flight or climb.

Note: Throughout this book the term 'autogiro' has been presented with the spelling used and originally patented as a Trade name by Cierva. It would be quite correct to use the term 'autogyro' but the alternative usage has been deliberately adopted as a tribute to Juan de Cierva, to recognise his status as a rotorcraft pioneer.

COMPOUND HELICOPTER

A rotorcraft which, in vertical or hovering flight, derives substantially the whole of its lift and control from a power-driven rotor system, whose axis (axes) is (are) approximately perpendicular to the longitudinal axis of the rotorcraft during such vertical or hovering flight, and in translational flight may derive a proportion of its lift, forward thrust or control from the embodiment of wings and/or propulsion systems.

CONVERTIPLANE

A rotorcraft which is capable of conversion during flight, so that lift is substantially or totally transferred from the rotors to other lifting devices such as fixed wings. A convertiplane will either incorporate a propulsive system to provide forward thrust, or may, as in the case of a tilt-rotor machine, re-configure the rotor to accept the role of a propeller.

AUTOROTATION

Autorotation may be defined as the condition of flight where the lifting rotor is driven in rotation by air forces, with no power being applied through the rotor shaft. Without power applied to the rotor, a conventional helicopter can be configured to operate in an autorotative descent, producing a power-off, manageable glide slope.

COLLECTIVE PITCH

Collective pitch is a process whereby incidence change is applied to all blades simultaneously, thereby providing a change in lift for the helicopter. This is achieved by movement of the collective lever.

CYCLIC PITCH

Cyclic pitch is the process whereby incidence changes can be applied to individual blades, in a cyclical manner, as they rotate around the azimuth. By this means blades can be made to vary around the rotor disc, effectively tilting the blade tip path plane, and thus the thrust vector. Control is achieved by movement of the cyclic control column, which allows the pilot to fly the helicopter in any chosen direction.

Introduction

The concept of the rotorcraft as a flying machine is as old as aviation itself. Indeed, the well-publicised studies by Leonardo da Vinci (1452–1519) are still regarded as the first serious attempt to consider the rotor as a practical means of achieving flight, and his drawings are frequently reproduced to symbolise the historical concept of the helicopter.

In fact, being an artist myself, I like to imagine that Leonardo was in his studio, explaining his idea to his model, Mona Lisa, as he worked, and that maybe this is the reason for her smile – she had just been told about the helicopter!

With the Industrial Revolution came the realisation that sustained flight was achievable. Most of the activity centred around wings and propellers, and the use of rotors as a primary means of achieving lift featured in many of the ideas, but, in general, the concept of the helicopter, capable of hovering and landing on a fixed point, was not fully appreciated.

Once steam power became available, inventors began to realise that the power to fly was within their grasp. But it was the invention of the internal combustion engine that really made it all possible.

The 'Miracle at Kitty hawk', as the Wright brothers' series of short flights in 1903 can rightfully be described, gave the world powered flight. But flight was still only achievable after a take-off run, or by means of some launching device to achieve flying speed; vertical take-off and landing proved to be illusive. Within four years of those first faltering steps into the air, several attempts were made to build rotorcraft. They were yet to be called helicopters.

Cierva's autogiros brought things a little closer, and unlocked the technology that made it possible for a rotorcraft to sustain flight and control through its rotor.

By the end of the Second World War helicopters were a definite reality. Not only was vertical take-off and controlled hovering achievable, but machines with this unique capability could be produced in quantity at an acceptable price.

Igor Sikorsky summed up the importance of the ability to hover when he stated that, 'If you are in trouble anywhere in the world, an airplane can fly over and drop flowers. A helicopter can land and save your life.'

With the war over, all thoughts turned to peaceful applications for the large aviation industry, which had been built up for wartime production. The helicopters of the day were neither large enough nor fast enough to be commercially viable for airline use. Only by applying a combination of available helicopter and aircraft technology did it seem possible to produce a vertical take-off airliner which might hold its own in the competitive airline market. The stage was set for the Rotodyne.

Rotodyne was a large compound helicopter, designed and built by the Fairey Aviation Company in the late 1950s. It was a bold concept, intended for production in the form of a 60,800lb, 27,579kg fifty-seven-seat VTOL airliner; and an even heavier version for military use, both of which combined helicopter and gyroplane technology to achieve forward speeds in excess of 200mph/321.87kph.

The most significant innovation in its design was the use of tip-jets. This book traces the origins of Fairey interest in tip-jet drive and the development of the successful 33.000lb/14,969kg, forty-seat demonstrator, which flew in 1957, and which, in the course of a four-year flight programme, proved the feasibility of the concept, and achieved all its experimental objectives.

When the Rotodyne project was terminated, in 1962, work was well underway on the design of the production aircraft; metal had been cut, a full-sized mock-up fuselage was built and development tests with the enlarged tip-jet system were in hand.

Because government finance and technical support had been involved throughout the programme, the prototype, hardware and data, were all deemed to be 'government property', and the disposal of such assets rested with 'officialdom'.

The end result was that the prototype was cut up and sold as scrap, and the design and development data was allowed to be carelessly dispersed, thus depriving the nation of valuable intellectual property.

A few years later, a similar fate befell the TSR-2 supersonic strike aircraft, and such activity has subsequently been held to be typical of British official thinking.

one

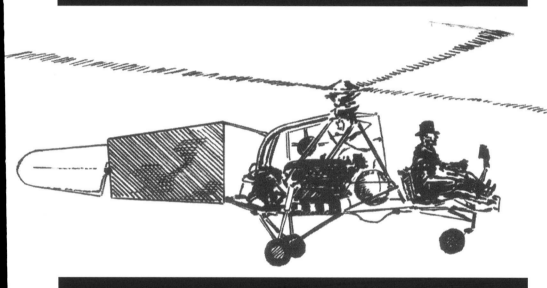

BEFORE THE ROTODYNE

The process whereby a helicopter rotor is driven by means of power units attached to the blade tips has always attracted rotorcraft designers. The advantages are obvious; by driving the rotor from the blade tips there is no resultant torque generated by a driven shaft, dispensing with the need for a gearbox between engine and rotor or any anti-torque system, such as a tail rotor.

Dispensing with the need for a mechanical drive system incorporating gearboxes offers the opportunity for substantial weight saving, and elimination of the tail rotor removes one of the helicopters most vulnerable features.

W.H. Phillips (1842)

As early as 1842, W.H. Phillips is reported to have flown a 2lb/1kg model helicopter, driven by steam effluxes from the blade tips, achieving limited success. Power was generated by burning a mixture of charcoal, gypsum and nitre (which, in the appropriate proportions, would produce gunpowder!).

Philips was a gentleman inventor who lived in Nunhead, in the Southwark area of south-east London, and is believed to have carried out this experiment on Primrose Hill.

The inventor described the event as follows:

> All being arranged, the steam was up in a few seconds, when the whole apparatus spun around like a top, and mounted into the air faster than a bird. To what height it ascended I had no means of ascertaining; the distance travelled was across two fields, where, after a long search, I found the machine minus its wings, which had been torn off in contact with the ground.

Reports of this flight vary as regards size and distance flown. There are no technical records of his work, and no record of a patent application, leaving it almost to the level of folklore, bereft of any formal recognition. If authenticated it would have been the first recorded powered flight, some six years before Stringfellow (1848). It would also have been the first recorded use of tip-jet drive, and the first successful steam-driven helicopter model.

It was reported that a replica of the Phillips model was placed on show at the exhibition held by the Royal Aeronautical Society at the Crystal Palace in 1868.

Louis Brennan (1924)

Brennan was, in fact, an Australian by birth, who established his reputation as an armaments engineer, with considerable success in torpedo design, and also by designing a gyro-stabilised monorail with military applications. As early as 1915 he had approached the War Office with proposals to produce a helicopter, and, to this end, a secret patent was taken out in his name.

The Brennan helicopter was achieving some success when it was discontinued by the Air Ministry in favour of Cierva's autogiros in 1926.

It was 1919 before any work commenced on the helicopter project. The Air Ministry established Brennan at Farnborough with all the facilities of the Royal Aircraft Factory at his disposal.

The Brennan helicopter was based around a rotary frame carrying two blades, driven by four-bladed propellers at the rotor tips. Power was provided by a single, horizontally mounted, Bentley BR 2 rotary engine of 230hp driving the two propellers through a gearbox, via shafts running the length of the blades.

The rotor diameter was 61ft/18.5m, and the blades had a chord of 6ft/2m. The structure rotated at 50/60rpm, and the all-up weight was 2764lb/1256kg. Brennan also designed an engine starting system for the aircraft.

The first flight took place in May 1924, piloted by R. Graham, who, like many of the early rotorcraft pilots, was not a professional aviator but an engineer who had 'greatness thrust upon him'. Subsequent flights consisted of brief hovers and limited transitions into low-speed forward flight. In the course of the two years that followed, over seventy flights, averaging three minutes each, were carried out, and significant progress was made in achieving stability and control.

The project was discontinued in 1926, upon the recommendation of the Air Ministry Aeronautical Research Committee, who saw no future in helicopters of the Brennan type, and advised that future rotary wing activities should be concentrated upon gyroplanes, such as Cierva's 'autogiro', which by this time was demonstrating spectacular success.

Brennan tried in vain to get the decision reversed. In his letter to the Air Ministry he said 'That the helicopter must and will come, I am now more convinced than when I started, and it is irresponsible for anyone to impede it'.

There were other attempts to use tip-drive:

Victor Isacco (Italy, 1926)

Isacco received support from the Air Ministry Directorate of Scientific Research, and accordingly placed a contract with Saunders-Roe to build a prototype of his machine 'Helicogyre No.3'.

The four-blade rotor was driven by four Bristol Cherub engines mounted at the blade tips, and a fifth engine was mounted in the nose of the aircraft to provide forward thrust. The finished aircraft was delivered to the Royal Aircraft Factory at Farnborough, but was found to be mechanically complex and unreliable, and never progressed beyond attempts to ground run.

Maitland Bleeker (USA, 1930)

In 1930, Maitland Bleeker, working with the Curtiss Company, built a tip-drive helicopter, where the rotor was driven by four propellers mounted at the blade tips, powered by a single engine mounted in the fuselage. The drive and control systems were complex, and although some 'uncertain' hovers were achieved, the project was abandoned at an early stage.

In the event, the main stream of helicopter development progressed along entirely different paths, the most familiar being the single main rotor, with torque offset by a smaller tail rotor that also provides yaw control, but the concept of tip-drive had been demonstrated and would be re-visited as technology progressed.

Juan de la Cierva (1926)

Before considering the Rotodyne, which was a compound helicopter capable of conversion to a gyroplane mode of operation, it is necessary understand some of the technology it utilised. Fundamental to its success was the ability to shut down the power to the tip-jets, allowing the rotor to autorotate, so that all the power from the engines was available to drive it through the air, the aircraft thus becoming a large gyroplane or 'autogiro'.

Juan de la Cierva started building aircraft as early as 1912, and in 1919 he turned his attention to the use of windmills, or rotors, as a means of sustaining lift at low speed. All aeroplanes are at risk of stalling, whereby they lose lift altogether. Indeed, it has always remained a primary cause of accidents, 'Watch your airspeed!' being the most common command given, with varying levels of urgency, by flying instructors since flying began. Cierva set out to produce a flying machine capable of flying at very low speeds, possibly eliminating the risk of stalling altogether.

In order to achieve this, he utilised the ability of the rotor to autorotate, whereby, at a suitable pitch setting, a rotor will continue to rotate without power, sustained by the torque equilibrium of the lift and drag forces acting on the blades. This phenomenon was already known, and in most modern helicopters it is available as a safety feature to allow controlled descent in the event of engine failure. With Cierva's gyroplane, the rotor was drawn through the air by means of a conventional propeller, with the result that the rotor generated sufficient lift to sustain level flight, climb and descent.

Before this could be satisfactorily achieved, Cierva experienced several failures, primarily associated with the unbalanced rolling movement generated when attempting take-off, due to asymmetry of lift between the advancing and retreating blades. This major difficulty was resolved by the introduction of the flapping hinge, whereby the blades, when subjected to such forces, could rise and fall accordingly, reducing the rolling force.

In January 1923, Lt Gomez Spencer flew Cierva's first successful autogiro at Getafe military airfield, near Madrid.

All Cierva's pioneering work was carried out in his native Spain. In 1925 he brought his C.6 to England and demonstrated it to the Air Ministry at Farnborough. This machine had a four-bladed rotor with flapping hinges, but relied upon conventional aircraft controls for pitch, roll and yaw. It was based upon the fuselage of an Avro 504K aeroplane; initial rotation of the rotor was achieved by the manual tension of a rope passed around stops on the undersides of the blades.

The Farnborough demonstration was a great success, and resulted in an invitation to continue work in the UK. As a direct result, the Cierva Autogiro Company was formed the following year. From the outset Cierva concentrated upon the design and the manufacture of rotor systems, relying on other established aircraft manufacturers to produce the airframes, predominately the A.V. Roe Company.

The Avro-built C.8 was basically a refinement of the C.6, with the more powerful 180hp Lynx radial engine, and several C.8s were built. The C.8R incorporated drag hinges, as it was found that the presence of flapping hinges caused blade oscillation in azimuth, giving rise to high stresses with the risk of blade failure. This brought on other problems, such as ground resonance, for which friction type drag dampers were fitted.

As the resolution of these fundamental rotor problems opened the way to progress, confidence built up rapidly, and, after several impressive cross-country flights, a C.8L was entered for the 1928 King Cup air race, and although it was forced to retire, it subsequently completed a 3,000-mile/4,800km tour of the British Isles. Later that year it flew from London to Paris, extending the tour to include Berlin, Brussels and Amsterdam, thus becoming the first rotating wing aircraft to cross the English Channel.

A predominant problem with the gyroplane was concerned with achieving initial rotor rotation. Several methods were attempted, in addition to the rope and drum system, which could take the rotor speed to 50 per cent of that required, at which point movement along the ground to reach flying speed was necessary, while tilting the rotor to establish autorotation.

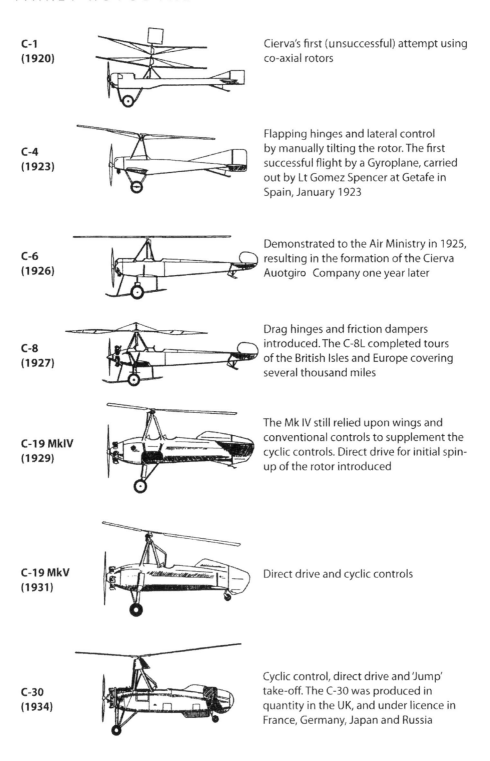

C-1
(1920)

Cierva's first (unsuccessful) attempt using co-axial rotors

C-4
(1923)

Flapping hinges and lateral control by manually tilting the rotor. The first successful flight by a Gyroplane, carried out by Lt Gomez Spencer at Getafe in Spain, January 1923

C-6
(1926)

Demonstrated to the Air Ministry in 1925, resulting in the formation of the Cierva Auotgiro Company one year later

C-8
(1927)

Drag hinges and friction dampers introduced. The C-8L completed tours of the British Isles and Europe covering several thousand miles

C-19 MkIV
(1929)

The Mk IV still relied upon wings and conventional controls to supplement the cyclic controls. Direct drive for initial spin-up of the rotor introduced

C-19 MkV
(1931)

Direct drive and cyclic controls

C-30
(1934)

Cyclic control, direct drive and 'Jump' take-off. The C-30 was produced in quantity in the UK, and under licence in France, Germany, Japan and Russia

Cierva's autogiros were the wonder of the 1930s. In solving the problems of rotor dynamics and control, Cierva paved the way to a practical helicopter.

Another approach was to tilt the tail stabiliser to deflect engine slipstream up through the rotor. The most acceptable solution was finally achieved with the C.19, which was produced in some quantities, with a direct drive from the engine to the rotor fitted, through which the rotor could be accelerated up to speed. The system was then declutched for the commencement of a very short take-off run.

As Cierva's autogiros achieved success and acceptance others began to follow, and with them came further innovation. Most important was the development of direct rotor control, which was achieved initially by tilting the rotor hub, and subsequently by the application of cyclic pitch, causing the blades to rise or fall at appropriate points in their rotation, thereby effectively tilting the rotor in the required direction.

The introduction of jump take-off was another major improvement in capability. The rotor was accelerated in fine pitch until the rotor speed required for flight was achieved. It was then declutched. The loss of torque caused the blades to swing forward on angled drag hinges, with a resultant increase in collective pitch causing the aircraft to leap into the air. With all the engine power applied to the forward-thrusting propeller, it was now possible to continue in forward flight with the rotor in autorotation.

All the above features were brought together in the C.30, which was produced in quantity for civil and military use, and the autogiros of the 1930s were looked upon as a wonder of their time. But it must however be emphasised that they were not helicopters, and were not capable of vertical take-off, landing or hovering in still air, albeit that they could maintain very low speed and accomplish a near vertical landing into wind.

The activities of the Cierva Company established a strong understanding of rotorcraft and rotor technology within the British aircraft industry, which was quickly taken up worldwide. A number of manufacturers produced aircraft for Cierva, including, Avro, Comper, de Havilland and Westland. Gyroplanes were built in many countries, including France, Germany, Japan, Russia and USA, using Cierva licences.

The importance of Cierva's work on rotors, and its effect upon the evolution of the helicopter, cannot be overstated, and is, indeed, recognised throughout the industry. In the process of creating the gyroplane (autogiro), Cierva established an understanding of rotor dynamics and control which was applicable to all rotorcraft, and undoubtedly led to the realisation of the helicopter.

It is interesting to note that although this work did lead the way to the helicopter, Cierva himself never set out to create such a machine. His primary interest was to produce an aircraft that could not stall. It is perhaps an ironic twist of fate that Cierva should die in an airline crash in 1936, while taking off from Croydon.

The Influence of German Activity

For further insight into the evolutionary process, it is necessary to look to Germany, where the potential of the helicopter was recognised long before a solution was realised. Several practical rotorcraft were flown in Germany during the years 1936–1945.

The progress achieved in Germany during the pre-war years is often symbolised by the image of the aviatrix, Hanna Reitsch, flying the twin-rotor Focke Achgelis Fa 61 in the Deutschlandhalle, Berlin, with apparent ease, in 1938.

There was, however, more than one helicopter project active in Germany, which incorporated some very innovative features and would subsequently apply to the Rotodyne.

Anton Flettner

The work of the German aeronautical engineer and inventor Anton Flettner is of special interest.

In the 1920s he proposed and successfully demonstrated a small ship utilising the 'Magnus effect', whereby the ship was driven as a result of air passing over large vertically mounted rotating cylinders. He was also the inventor of the 'rotary ventilator', commonly seen on vans and other vehicles as a means of providing ventilation and cooling.

When Flettner first turned his interest to helicopters in 1930, he designed an aircraft with a single, torqueless rotor driven by two 30hp Anzani engines driving two small propellers attached to the blades. Unfortunately the prototype was destroyed whilst undergoing tethered testing.

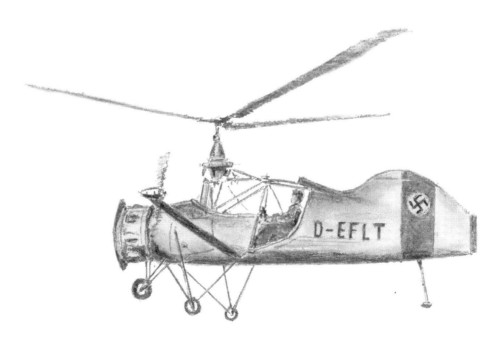

The Flettner Fl 185 demonstrated a practical helicopter that could convert to gyroplane mode as early as 1937.

Flettner then produced and successfully flew a very elegant gyroplane, in 1936, but the sole prototype was lost as the result of an in-flight fire.

Flettner's interest was then directed towards a rotorcraft designed to operate as a helicopter when power was applied to the rotor, but the rotor could be de-clutched allowing the aircraft to operate as a gyroplane, with the rotor in autorotation during forward flight. This was accomplished by means of two propellers mounted on outriggers, operating in opposite directions, to counteract torque and provide yaw control in the helicopter regime. Once in forward flight, the rotor was declutched allowing it to autorotate, and both propellers were re-adjusted to provide forward thrust, thus converting to a gyroplane. Designated the Flettner Fl 185, a single prototype was built and flown with limited success.

Flettner continued his interest in helicopters, and designed his ingenious twin intermeshing rotor system, which he used for his Flettner Fl 265. Because it used two contra-rotating rotors, torque reaction was no longer a problem and, as a consequence, there was no requirement for a complex outrigger propeller system. The Fl 265 functioned as a pure helicopter, deriving its forward thrust and control directly from the rotors.

Six Fl 265 test aircraft were built and used in an extensive programme to assess helicopter applications, working with submarines, ships and ground troops. The trials were of sufficient success for the high command to agree to quantity production, but, by this time, work was well advanced on the two-seat Flettner Fl 282 Kolibri, which did achieve quantity production after undergoing operational trials in the Baltic with the German Navy, after the war had ended. Twenty-four prototype and pre-production aircraft had been completed, and a large production order had been placed.

Flettner's helicopter work provided early demonstrations of features that would be part of the Rotodyne's flight profile.

Friedrich von Doblhoff

The Wiener Neustadter Flugzeugwerke (WNF) was a major aircraft works situated close to Vienna, and which was mainly concerned with the production of Messerschmitt Bf 109 fighters for the Luftwaffe, producing as many as 270 aircraft per month.

Friedrich von Doblhoff was a senior designer with the organisation when he turned his attention to helicopters, and was given permission to set up a small team to advance his ideas. From the outset, Doblhoff favoured the use of tip-jet drive because of its apparent simplicity, and the fact that such a system required no correction for rotor torque.

It was a bold step indeed to undertake the development of a jet-driven helicopter, when rotorcraft were still in their infancy, and only a few years after the first successful turbojet powered flight, with the Heinkel He 178.

The programme was designated WNF342, and work commenced in October 1942 with the construction of a prototype WNF342 V1. Power was provided by a single 60hp Walter Mikron engine driving a compressor in order to provide air for the

Doblhoff built and flew the world's first jet-driven helicopter only a few years after the first jet engine, with a rotor driven by tip-jets; there were no problems arising from torque reaction. The WNF 342 V1 is seen here piloted by Stepan on its first flight.

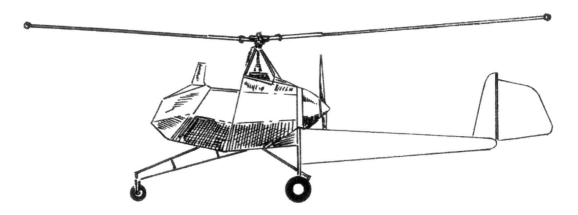

The WNF342 V4 was a two-seater, intended to demonstrate the ability to convert from helicopter to gyroplane. The war ended before this work could be undertaken.

tip-jets. Once mixed with petrol, the fuel/air mixture was passed through the rotor head to the tip-jets and ignited, generating a high-velocity efflux to drive the rotor.

Prototypes V1 and V2 were not provided with feathering hinges, and relied upon power variation, affecting the rotor speed in order to control the hover. Attitude and yaw control was achieved by means of downwash and airflow passing over moveable sections on the rear fuselage. Both the prototypes flew well enough to impress the Luftwaffe, ensuring continued support.

The third prototype, V3, was of a totally different configuration, sporting a twin-boom layout with aerodynamic controls for pitch and yaw. The power system was similar to that used with the earlier machines, but was fitted with a more powerful 140hp BMW engine to drive the compressor, which delivered air for the tip-jets when operating as a helicopter. Once forward flight had been achieved the rotor jets could be extinguished, and power transferred by means of a clutch to drive a pusher propeller.

The first flight with aircraft V1 took place in the spring of 1943. The results achieved with V1, V2 and V3 were sufficiently promising to ensure support from the German High Command, but all were subject to the common helicopter problems of vibration and resonance, which were to eventually destroy V3.

The construction of a fourth prototype, V4, was sanctioned, and this was larger and much more sophisticated than its predecessors, being a two-seater with a rotor diameter of 33ft/10m, and included a collective pitch control system.

The flight profiles tested on V3 and V4 laid the foundations for the Rotodyne, even though the German programme was slow due to Allied raids, and although satisfactory transitions into forward flight were achieved, a full flight envelope was not explored before the end of hostilities stopped further activity.

Two of the aircraft, V2 and V4, were quickly moved to Zell am See, an area which fell within the American zone, putting the aircraft and technical team into Allied hands.

One of the leading figures in the Doblhoff group was the young engineer, *Dipl Ing* August Stepan. Once the first aircraft had progressed towards flight, it was Stepan who was elected to be the test pilot. Besides being technically qualified to undertake this task; he was also the smallest and lightest member of the team (worth his lack of weight in gold!). Stepan played his pioneering role with distinction and courage, surviving several serious incidents.

With the war over, the aircraft fell into American hands and were promptly shipped to the USA, accompanied by Doblhoff himself, who later joined McDonnell Aircraft to continue his work, playing a leading part in the McDonnell XV-1 programme.

The XV-1 was a small compound helicopter, powered by a 550hp Continental engine, which drove a compressor to provide air for tip-jets mounted on a three-bladed rotor. In this mode it operated as a helicopter. Once level flight was achieved, the tip-jets could be extinguished, and the aircraft could then operate as a gyroplane. There was a third mode, known as the 'airplane mode', where the rotor would be set to minimum pitch in autorotation, no longer contributing lift, the craft now relying on its wings to sustain flight.

The first of two aircraft, weighing only 5,510lb/2504kg, flew in early 1954, and the programme continued until 1957, during which time a speed of 199mph/320.26kph was achieved, making it the first rotorcraft to approach 200mph. The project never progressed beyond the 'experimental' stage.

Stepan and another member of the Doblhoff team, *Dipl Ing* von Czernin, came to the UK to join the Fairey Aviation Company, which was beginning to develop an interest in tip–jet drive for a projected large transport helicopter, which was to eventually emerge as the Rotodyne.

SO 1221 Djinn

Another member of the Doblhoff team, Theodor Laufer, was absorbed into the French helicopter industry, working for the nationalised Societe Nationale de Constructions Aeronautique Sud-Ouest (SNCASO), where he played a leading role in the design and development of the little Djinn helicopter.

The Djinn has the distinction of being the only tip–jet-drive helicopter to achieve quantity production, and to enter service in any numbers. Powered by a single 250hp Turbomeca Palouste, it relied upon a 'cold–air' bleed to the blade tips to drive the rotor. Yaw control was achieved by deflection off a stainless steel fin situated in the jet efflux.

Two prototypes (SO 1220) were built for the test programme, the first flight taking place in 1953, followed by over 150 production machines (SO 1221), most of which saw service with the French armed forces, with a substantial number being used for agriculture.

The Fairey Aviation Company

The Fairey Aviation Company was one of many aircraft manufacturing groups that came into being to meet the demand for aircraft during the First World War.

Richard Fairey, then chief engineer at Short Brothers, formed the company in 1915. He was just twenty-eight years old when he established his works in a leased factory at Hayes in Middlesex, not far from what is now the site of Heathrow Airport. Initially, Fairey built Short seaplanes and Sopwith 1½ Strutters, but as the war progressed a design office was established and a range of Fairey-designed seaplanes and flying boats came into being. By the end of the war a large purpose-built factory had been established at North Hyde Road, Hayes.

The company grew during the years between the wars to become a major aircraft manufacturer, with factories at Stockport and Hamble, responsible for many famous aircraft. The Fairey Aviation Company established a fine reputation as the manufacturer of naval aircraft, including such famous types as Swordfish, Fulmar, Firefly and Gannet.

During the Second World War the British aircraft industry had grown to massive proportions, and by the end of hostilities it was evident that the industry would have to operate within a totally different commercial structure, without the guarantee of easily acquired military contracts that had prevailed throughout the war. As events turned out in the uncertain peacetime years that followed, the onset of the Cold War did create a need for military aircraft.

The Fairey Company was fully occupied with production of the Firefly derivatives, and development of the Gannet for the Royal Navy. A separate division had also been established to develop guided weapons, involving a whole new field of technology.

It had, however, became clear that the industry would have to adapt to meet the requirements of civil aviation, working in an area where demand was growing rapidly, and the potential of the helicopter was recognised in a market with a whole new spectrum of peacetime applications, with the promise of expansion as the unique capabilities of the helicopter were realised.

The decision was made to expand the company's activities to include the design and manufacture of helicopters. A strong helicopter design team was formed, under the leadership of Dr J.A.J. Bennet, and it was decided to concentrate on original designs rather than follow the commercially safer path to build established types under licence.

Gyrodyne

The Fairey team took an innovative approach from the outset. Departing from the tail rotor configuration, which most contemporary helicopter designs favoured, Fairey elected to use a forward-thrusting propeller mounted on the starboard stub wing, 9ft/2.74m from the centreline, to offset rotor torque, the variable pitch propeller also served as a yaw control, whilst providing some additional forward thrust to drive the aircraft through the air. The Gyrodyne could be described as a compound helicopter, with its short stub wings, which did contribute some lift in forward flight. The use of the propeller to provide the primary source of forward thrust for the Gyrodyne effectively offloaded the main rotor in level flight conditions. Thus it was that the Fairey design used compound features as a means of keeping rotor loads and vibration levels down, rather than simply as a means of achieving high speeds.

The control system was arranged so that the throttle and collective pitch application were linked in a single control lever, eliminating the then familiar twist-grip commonly used on most helicopters of the period. Once in forward flight, yaw control was maintained by means of aerodynamic rudders, and attitude trim was maintained through an elevator.

Power was provided by a 520hp Alvis Leonides nine-cylinder radial engine driving a 51ft 9in/15.62m rotor, which was substantially larger than that of the Westland Dragonfly, which measured 48ft/14,63m, whilst the Gyrodyne's maximum all-up weight was 4,800lb/2,177kg, compared with 5,870lb/2,622kg. All this resulted in a comparatively low rotor disc loading.

The Gyrodyne flew for the first time from the company's flight test airfield at White Waltham on 7 December 1947, in the hands of the chief helicopter test pilot, Squadron Leader Basil Arkell. In June 1948, the Gyrodyne claimed a helicopter world speed record, achieving an average speed of 124.3mph/200.04kph along a two-way course adjacent to White Waltham.

The Fairey Gyrodyne was an attractive and potentially fast helicopter aimed at the post-war market. Development was discontinued after a disastrous crash.

The development task was progressing well, and a second aircraft was about to join the programme when the prototype crashed, following a rotor head failure near Reading, killing the pilot F.H Dixon, and his flight test observer, D. Garroway.

The subsequent investigation showed that the failure was due to metal fatigue, and as a result work on the project was discontinued.

Jet Gyrodyne

From the outset of its activity with helicopters, Fairey maintained an abiding interest in tip-jet drive, with a particular interest in the system that had been so effectively demonstrated by Doblhoff. With this in mind, members of the Doblhoff team (including August Stepan) were invited to join the company, and given a free hand to continue research into jet units.

The focal point of this activity was the establishment of a static testing site in the remote north-west corner of White Waltham airfield, where facilities for static running in fully instrumented test cells, and a spinning rig for dynamic testing, were built. Working from the design office at Hayes, and the White Waltham test site, the Fairey Jet research group designed and tested a range of pressure jet systems, which would emerge on the ultra-light helicopter and the Rotodyne.

Following the loss of the prototype Gyrodyne in 1949, the second aircraft became available for use as a test vehicle. The basic shape of the Gyrodyne was retained, as was the Alvis Leonides nine-cylinder radial engine. This was adapted to drive two Rolls-Royce Merlin compressors, which provided air for the tip-jets. The engine also provided power for two variable pitch pusher propellers, mounted on the tips of the stub wings.

The second Gyrodyne was converted to accept tip-jet drive and was used to prove the practicality of transition from helicopter to gyroplane mode in advance of the Rotodyne.

The 'Jet Gyrodyne', as it was named, had a large 60ft/18.29m–diameter, two–blade, fully articulated rotor with cyclic and collective pitch controls. The kerosene-burning pressure jets were mounted tangentially at the blade tips, air from the compressors was ducted to the jet units through the rotor head and blades, to be mixed with vaporised fuel, and, once ignited, the jet units remained in a self-sustaining state, power being controlled by variation of the fuel/air mixture.

A long cautious programme was drawn up to demonstrate the flight regime that was finally adopted for the Rotodyne: the rotor would be run up on air-only and then following the introduction of fuel, 'ignition' selected. With the jets burning the aircraft could be flown as a helicopter, control, lift and forward thrust being derived from the rotor, whilst yaw control was available through differential pitch, applied to the two pusher propellers.

Once in forward flight the tip–jets were extinguished and the rotor allowed to establish itself in autorotation, the compressors were then de–clutched and full power became available to the two propellers. With the rotor settled in an autorotative condition, and with the jets extinguished, the Jet Gyrodyne was operating as a gyroplane, the rotor providing most of its lift with a small contribution from the stub wings. In this condition, the two pusher propellers maintained forward thrust. The twin fins provided yaw control, which could be supplemented by application of differential propeller pitch. The aircraft was a true compound helicopter, incorporating a refinement of the features demonstrated by Flettner and Doblhoff.

The Jet Gyrodyne flew for the first time in January 1954, flown by Fairey test pilot John Dennis, and operating under a Ministry contract as a research vehicle. The main purpose of the programme was to develop and demonstrate the operation of a jet-driven helicopter, and to investigate the process of 'transition' from helicopter (jets burning) to gyroplane (jets out). There was also, of course, the need to prove that the Fairey-designed tip-jets offered a viable means of power for a helicopter.

Testing to establish a safe transition technique had to be approached with caution; the modified Gyrodyne was underpowered for its weight of 6,000lb/2,722kg, and the whole process was affected by the permutation of forward speed, rotor speed, propeller pitch, control, jet response and light–up.

The first phase of testing to assess the aircraft as a jet-driven helicopter went very well, and the process of conversion from flight as a helicopter to the gyroplane regime also proved to be straightforward, within the constraints of experimental test flying.

The transition from helicopter to gyroplane benefited from one of the in–built safety features of the autogiro; the fact that, once in autorotation, the aircraft could complete a low speed run-on landing without risk. Most of the transition testing was carried out in the proximity of the airfield.

Reversal, involving a transition back to the helicopter regime, proved to be a much more difficult operation, frequently accompanied by an unacceptable loss of height, and autorotative landings were not uncommon.

Gradually an understanding of the required flight conditions was gained, and the reliability of the tip-jet units, particularly with reference to light-up, improved, such that the full transition process, without serious height loss, could be confidently demonstrated, as indeed it was during the 1955 SBAC display at Farnborough.

By late 1956, the design of the Rotodyne was well advanced, and construction of the prototype had commenced. Transitions were being undertaken with confidence, and the aircraft was flown by a number of pilots, not least the nominated test crew for the Rotodyne itself.

The importance of the work carried out with the Jet Gyrodyne cannot be overstated. In the course of the test programme, over 190 transitions were successfully completed, and the process fully understood. The direct result was that the Rotodyne programme was able to proceed with confidence, and that the design objectives were achievable within an acceptable margin of safety.

The Fairey Ultra-Light

The British procurement authorities had been notoriously slow to appreciate the value of the helicopter in the battlefield. The Battle of the Imjin River, which occurred during the Korean War, in 1951, when the Gloucestershire Regiment was pinned down by a Chinese offensive, brought home the fact that evacuation and supply could have been accomplished with helicopters had they been available.

The Fairey Ultra-Light relied upon tip-jet drive, and was intended for service with the army and navy. It was extremely agile, but proved to be too small to meet the requirement for the British forces.

During 1953 Fairey responded to Air Ministry and Ministry of Supply requests for a small helicopter for use as an observation platform by the army. The company proposed a light tip-jet-driven helicopter, in the form of its diminutive Ultra-Light; a small two-seat helicopter, weighing only 1,800lb/817kg fully loaded, with a rotor diameter of 28ft/6.61m, which relied solely upon tip-jets to power the rotor, directional control being achieved through a stainless steel fin placed directly in the efflux of the 250hp Turbomeca Palouste, and which could be moved, via the rudder pedals, to direct the efflux left or right, thus steering the helicopter.

The prototype was flown for the first time in August 1955 by W.R. Gellatly, who had been appointed chief helicopter test pilot, later to be joined by J.G.P. Morton. The Ultra-light was remarkably manoeuvrable, and gave many impressive demonstrations at the Farnborough Air Show, landing and taking off from the back of a moving flatbed lorry

Fairey also proposed the aircraft for shipborne use, and sea trials were carried out, operating from a small deck specially fitted to the frigate HMS *Grenville*. Although the trials both at sea and with the army were proclaimed a success, the services made it clear that the requirement was for a substantially larger aircraft, and withdrew support.

In spite of the fact that UK military interest had evaporated, Fairey continued with the development programme at full pace, accompanied by a vigorous marketing campaign. There was a hope for American interest when the Piasecki Aircraft Corporation applied for an option to build for the US Army, but this failed to materialise.

The White Waltham test-rigs were fundamental to the development of the Ultra-Light, and a fully functioning airframe was committed for use as a spinning rig for maturity testing. The Ultra-Light programme was still in progress when the Rotodyne flew in 1957 and continued until the project was finally abandoned in 1959.

two

THE ROTODYNE THAT
WAS BUILT AND FLOWN

Fairey Type 'Y'

The decision to use tip-jets as the main means for rotor power was made quite early in the evolution of Fairey as a helicopter company, and it was as a result of this decision that key members of the Doblhoff team were employed as soon as they became available.

With the Second World War over, the large British aircraft industry was eager to adapt to peacetime applications. The Fairey Company decided that there was a place in the market for a large transport helicopter, which they elected to call 'Rotodyne'.

Air transportation in the 1950s suffered from the same problem as that which besets the air traveller today; the simple fact that, at least for short journeys, transport to the airport, check-in times and the positioning of the aircraft for take-off, often takes longer than the flight itself.

The Fairey team worked on a premise that the helicopter, with its vertical take-off capability, given increased cruising speed, would have a distinct advantage over faster fixed wing aeroplanes. The main case for helicopter or Rotodyne operation, as opposed to fixed-wing aircraft, was that as VTOL aircraft they could operate from city-centre to city-centre, once central heliports had been established.

Check-in time would be common to both, but the journey to the airport, which by its nature must be situated well away from the centre, could be at least one hour, to which must be added the time for a normal airliner to get to its take-off point on the runway. All this could result in anything up to three hours being added to a journey from London to Paris, where the actual flight time would be little more than one hour.

The average speed of an aircraft such as the Viscount was approximately 300mph/480kph. A Rotodyne, cruising at 150mph/240kph, could still take passengers from city-centre to city-centre in considerably less time. The potential market lay in Europe and the north-eastern states of America, where the distance between city-centres is generally less than 200 miles/320km.

Following the end of the Second World War, most of the European airlines were extensively equipped with surplus military aircraft adapted for civil use, the predominant type being the Douglas DC-3/C-47 Dakota, which, as a civil aircraft, could carry between twenty and thirty passengers. It was clear that most of these aircraft provided only an interim solution, and would have to be replaced fairly promptly. It was considered by the Fairey team that a large helicopter, which could take full advantage of its vertical take-off capability to operate directly out of city-centres, could fill a substantial part of this market.

The 'Brabazon Committee' was formed in 1943 to investigate the future needs of the British airliner market; the group identified a range of aircraft to meet long-haul and short-haul requirements. By 1950 the British industry was responding with a number of projects, which were to materialise in the form of some well-known aircraft such as the de Havilland Dove, Airspeed Ambassador, Vickers Viscount, Bristol Britannia, de Havilland Comet and the mighty Brabazon.

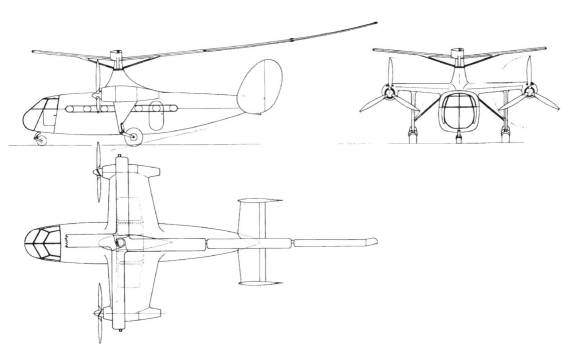

The original proposal in 1950, offering a rotorcraft with twenty-seat capacity and a fixed undercarriage, and powered by two Rolls-Royce Dart engines.

As early as 1947 the Fairey Company submitted a proposal to the Ministry of Supply, who at the time were responsible for procurement, offering a compound helicopter capable of carrying twenty passengers, with a four-bladed rotor powered by two Rolls-Royce Dart engines.

British European Airways responded immediately with a request for a larger aircraft capable of carrying twenty-eight passengers, comparable with their existing equipment. As time progressed the configuration of the next generation of airliners became clear, and aircraft capable of carrying forty passengers were in the process of being developed, powered by turboprops resulting in cruising speeds as high as 300mph/480kph.

All this resulted in a flow of proposals for a rotorcraft with more capacity and which was capable of higher cruising speeds. By 1953 the proposed Rotodyne had evolved into an aircraft with provision for forty passengers and a cruising speed of 165mph/265kph, considerably higher than that achieved by its contemporaries, and sufficient to maintain the advantage offered by 'city-centre to city-centre' operations.

The configuration finally offered and accepted took the form of a truncated fixed wing airliner, powered by two Napier Eland E.L.7 propeller turbines, developing 3,250shp. This was surmounted by a 90ft/27.4m-diameter four-blade rotor, driven by tip-jets, which drew air from an auxiliary compressor mounted in tandem with the Eland installation, connected by a clutch for the helicopter phase of operations.

The response from British European Airways, in 1952, was for a larger aircraft capable of carrying forty passengers, and was powered by two Rolls-Royce Dart and two DH engines.

The proposal for a forty-seat version, powered by two Napier Eland engines, which was accepted by British European Airways.

A contract for approximately £780,000 was finally awarded, in July 1953, to cover the construction of a prototype of the forty-seat aircraft, to meet the requirements of British European Airways. The new aircraft took the Fairey Aviation designation 'Type Y', to be known as 'The Fairey Rotodyne'.

Government involvement in the project also implied the possibility of military applications, and throughout its development the Rotodyne carried the military serial number XE521.

Airframe

Throughout the design of the basic airframe every effort was made to produce an aircraft of simple robust construction, bearing in mind the overriding importance of maintenance, servicing, repair and overhaul, which constitute so large a factor in operating economy.

The Rotodyne under construction at the Hayes factory in 1957.

The low operating altitude meant that there was no requirement for cabin pressurization, which in turn made it possible to provide large windows spaced in line with each row of seats, a luxury not normally available to passengers.

Light alloy stressed skin construction was used throughout, and all major components were built as separate units readily detachable from one another by simple bolted joints.

Fuselage

Construction of the fuselage took the form of a semi-monocoque structure with four longerons and vertical frames of pressed light alloy sheet. The fuselage held a constant

An internal view of the main fuselage during construction, looking aft towards the two large clamshell doors.

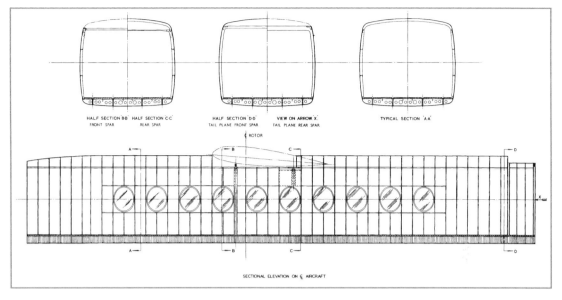

The main fuselage structure was uncomplicated, facilitating ease of production. The 6ft of headroom would have been very popular with passengers.

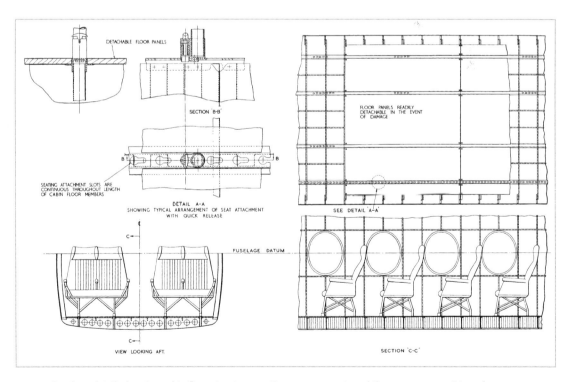

Fuselage detail, showing cabin floor structure, seating arrangement, and the generous provision of windows.

cross-section from the crew entry door to the rear freight loading doors, thus enabling a large number of frames of identical design to be used. Double curvature of the skin panels was also avoided, aimed at keeping manufacturing costs to a minimum.

In order to allow the wing to pass over the top of the fuselage as one continuous structure, a recess was formed in the top of the fuselage, into which the wing sat, attached to suitably strengthened frames by a pair of pick-up bolts on the front and rear spars.

The floor of the cabin was carried on the fuselage frames, which were increased in depth to take all bending loads to each side of the fuselage. Intercostal stiffeners were spaced between the frames to reduce the size of unsupported floor area. The floor was made up of readily detachable panels of sandwich construction, which were easily replaceable in the event of damage.

At the rear, the fuselage structure terminated in a frame immediately aft of the horizontal tail surface. From this point the fuselage fairing was completed by a pair of clamshell doors, carried on vertical hinges from the rear fuselage frame, and arranged to open hydraulically. The tailplane was mounted on top of the fuselage at the extreme rear of the main structure, just ahead of the clamshell doors, and was attached by bolts at the front and rear spars.

Wing

The wing was a stressed skin-covered construction with two main spars; it was of constant thickness and chord. The two main spars, which were continuous from tip to tip, ran

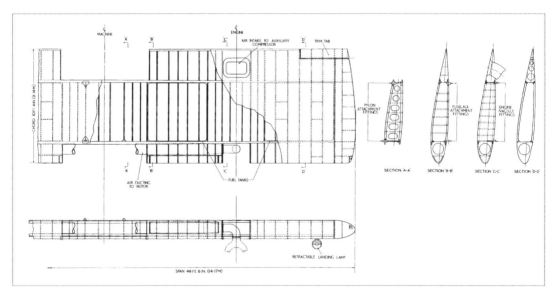

The wing provided approximately 50 per cent of the lift when operating in gyroplane mode. It also contained all the main fuel tankage (726 gallons/3,300ltrs).

parallel in the plan, and were made of sheet web, with an extruded boom construction throughout. The wing ribs were constructed from pressed light alloy sheet.

The wing was attached to the fuselage at four points, and provision was made on the front and rear spars for the pick-ups of the rotor pylon structure.

Provision was made for fuel to be carried in four tanks, arranged between the wing spars, one inboard 170 gallons/773ltrs, and one 193 gallons/877ltrs outboard of each engine nacelle, all feeding to a 30 gallon/136ltrs collector tank, situated in the pylon.

The leading edge of the wing, inboard of the nacelles, was built up of full-depth pressed plate ribs, suitably cut away to house the tip-jet air ducting, forward of which was a sub-spar.

Between this sub-spar and the extreme leading edge, a tunnel was formed through which all services to the engines passed.

Tail Unit

The tailplane was of constant chord and thickness, and was mounted on the rear fuselage such that it could be readily detached by the removal of four bolts. Construction was of light alloy throughout, with front and rear spars built up of plate webs and extruded booms, the structure being formed with pressed sheet alloy ribs.

Attachment points were provided at the outboard ends of tailplane spars for the vertical fins and rudders. The horizontal stabiliser was fitted with elevators.

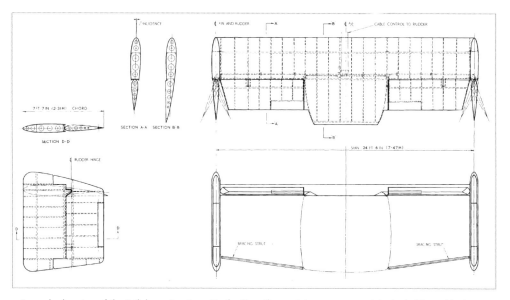

An early drawing of the tailplane structure. By the time the prototype was completed wind tunnel tests had shown that additional fin area was required and the upper fins were fitted.

Fairey, now part of the Westland Group, re-designated the aircraft 'Type FA-1'. It is perhaps interesting to note that up until this time the production aircraft had been known as 'Type Z', and maybe it was prophetic that Fairey type designations, having started at 'A' and continued alphabetically, reached the end of the alphabet just as the Westland takeover took place.

It was to have been a big aircraft as the following comparison illustrates:

	Military ROTODYNE	CH 47 Chinook
All-up Weight	68.300lb/30,980kg	54,000lb/24,495kg
Cabin Length	47ft/14.3m	30ft/9.1m
Width	9ft/2.8m	7.5ft/2.3m
Height	7ft/2.13m	6.5ft/1.9m

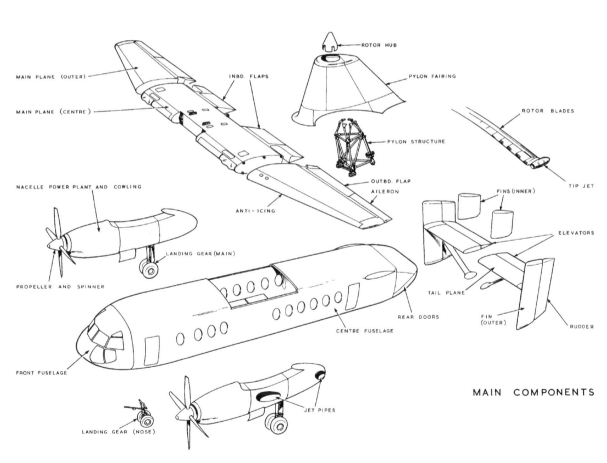

MAIN COMPONENTS

The Rotodyne 'Type Z' (FA-1) military version, showing the main components.

Undercarriage

The Fairey Rotodyne was fitted with a fully retracting wide track 24ft 6in/7.47m undercarriage. Each main undercarriage leg consisted of a single oleo-pneumatic shock absorber strut carrying twin wheels on a common axle. The main wheels retracted aft by hydraulic power into the engine nacelles. The twin nose wheel unit was a single oleo pneumatic strut mounted at the base of the bulkhead immediately aft of the pilot's control cabin, retracting forward by means of a single hydraulic jack.

The system was fitted with hydraulically operated disc-type brakes, which could be operated independently by toe pedals, or collectively by means of a hand parking lever.

The Fairey-designed undercarriage had to be capable of taking normal helicopter loads and dynamic inputs. Runway landings and taxiing were also a part of the requirement.

The undercarriage-operating lever was situated to be accessible to both pilots; in the event of a hydraulic failure it was possible to release the undercarriage from its up locks and effect full landing gear deployment with correct locking by gravity.

Provision was made to prevent inadvertent retraction of the undercarriage while the aircraft was on the ground.

Hydraulic System

The main hydraulic system had two pumps for the main source of supply, one for each engine. In a large helicopter, such as the Rotodyne, control is totally dependent upon hydraulic power. A duplicate system was provided, with an independent source of supply, using a pump mounted on a gearbox driven directly from the rotor head and located in the main rotor pylon. The two systems functioned continuously in parallel to ensure full control could be maintained even in the unlikely event of a double engine failure.

The hydraulic system also powered undercarriage retraction and lowering and wheel brakes.

The Passenger Cabin

On entering the Rotodyne, a passenger would be confronted with a comfortable, well-appointed airline environment, with ample headroom, typical of, if not better than, any medium airliner then in service. Seats were arranged in pairs each side of a central gangway.

The main passenger cabin was 33ft/10m long, 8ft/2.44m wide and 6ft/1.83m high. Provision was made for forty passengers, with a seat pitching of 36in/91.5cm, and included a small pantry for light in-flight catering, and a toilet compartment. The central gangway was 13in/33cm wide, with a level, unobstructed floor.

Window spacing was generous, in the form of ten large elliptical windows measuring 25in/63.5cm by 21in/53.3cm, so all passengers had an excellent all-round view. In the case of the demonstrator aircraft (XE521), which was an experimental aircraft, only the rear half of the cabin was fitted out with passenger accommodation for twenty passengers. The forward area accommodated the flight test crew and test equipment.

Entry to the cabin came via a spacious 'airstair' door measuring 5.85ft/1.8m by 3ft/0.91m, with an easy ascent up a few steps to the cabin floor, less than 4ft above ground level. The rear fuselage was fitted with large clamshell doors, provided primarily for the freight or car ferry role, and which, when used, would provide unobstructed entrance to the cabin.

An air-conditioning system was also to be provided to ensure passenger comfort in operating conditions ranging from –10°C to 35°C.

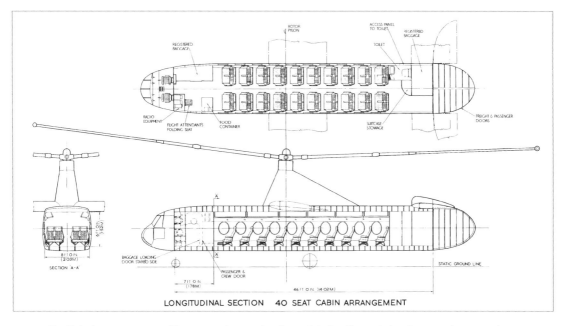

The Rotodyne passenger cabin was spacious and well appointed, with ample headroom and generously sized windows for each row of seats.

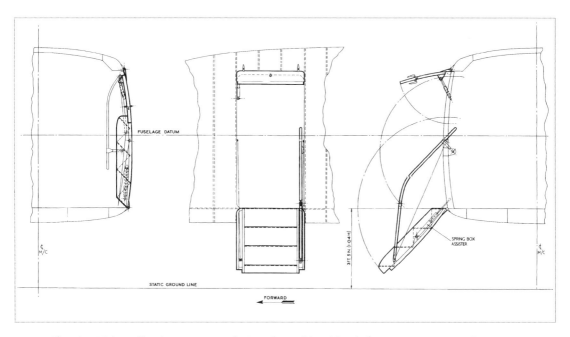

The 'airstair' door offered easy access to the Rotodyne cabin, with only four easy steps to negotiate to reach the cabin floor, which was less than 4ft from ground level.

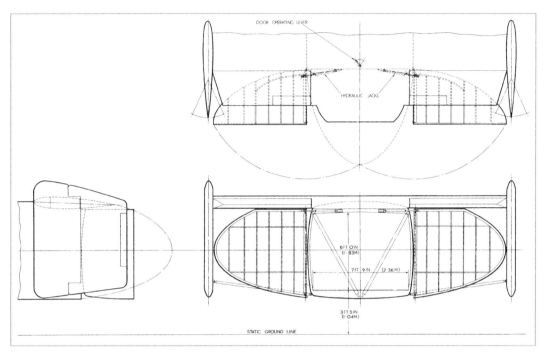

The large hydraulically operated 'clamshell' doors offered total access to the cabin for the freight role. The Rotodyne was seen as a strong contender for operation on the cross-Channel car-ferry routes, which were very active in the 1960s.

The cockpit of XE521 included a lot of additional test instrumentation but, even so, offered superb all-round vision. The proposed layout for the production aircraft can be seen on page 112.

Pilot's Cabin

The pilot's control cabin was provided for two pilots seated side by side, such that the aircraft could be operated from either seat. The flying controls followed the normal conventional helicopter layout of cyclic control and collective lever.

The all-round vision for the pilots was generously provided for by large glazed panels, including overhead transparencies, to allow for observation of the area directly above the aircraft. Clear panels were also provided around the underside of the nose, such that the ground directly under the aircraft would be visible during landing, in keeping with normal helicopter practice.

The Main Rotor Head Assembly

The main rotor head for the Rotodyne differed considerably from that of a conventional helicopter. Because the rotor was driven from within itself by means of tip-jets, there was no requirement for a gearbox, direct engine input or any transmission system for a tail-rotor.

There were, however, complex arrangements for passing air, fuel and high-energy electrical power for ignition, through the rotor head and blades to the tip-jets.

Compressed air for the tip-jets was generated by the auxiliary-compressors mounted on the aft end of the Napier Eland Turboprops. The air was ducted along the leading

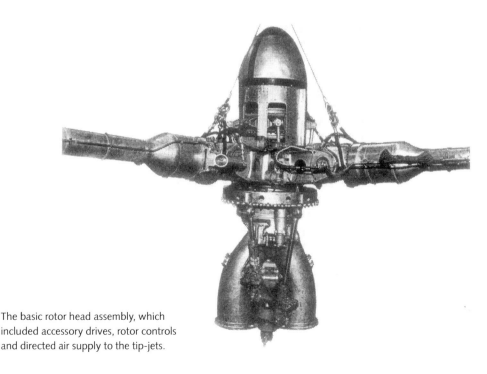

The basic rotor head assembly, which included accessory drives, rotor controls and directed air supply to the tip-jets.

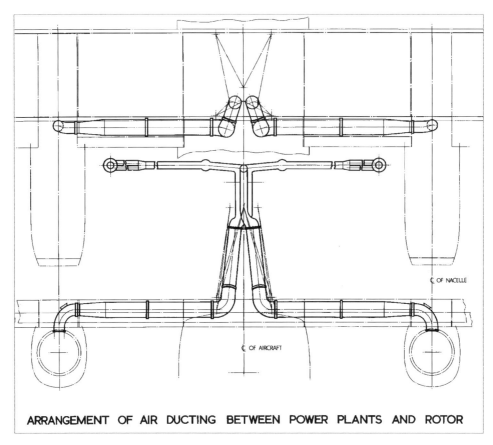

ARRANGEMENT OF AIR DUCTING BETWEEN POWER PLANTS AND ROTOR

The rotor assembly was different from conventional helicopters in that there was no gearbox with direct input from the engines as such. The drive system took air from the auxiliary-compressors through ducting to the rotor head assembly.

edge of the wings and up into the rotor pylon. The ducting merged at this point, with the two separate sources of air kept separate to form two concentric rings around a central shaft which housed the rotor controls and tip–jet fuel and electrical services. This part of the assembly was generally known as the 'trouser legs'.

The upper part of the ducting assembly continued in its concentric form to direct air to diametrically opposite pairs of blades, each pair of blades receiving air from one of the two engines, thus ensuring that in the event of a single engine failure air supply could be maintained to provide power on one pair of rotor blades.

The upper part of the assembly was of course rotating, whilst the lower half was fixed; the two halves being joined by gas–tight rotating seals.

The entire ducting arrangement was assembled with the rotor head, the rotor controls passing down through the centre, and the control runs passing from the rotating swash plate situated above the rotor head to the fixed control assembly housed at the base of the trouser leg arrangement.

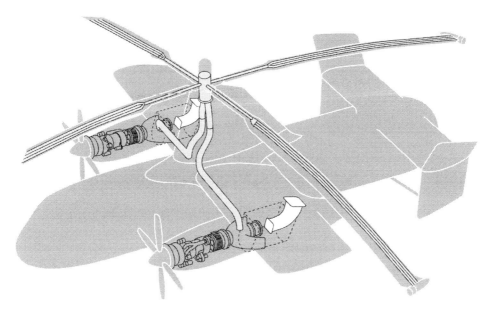

A diagrammatic layout of the complete Rotodyne power system.

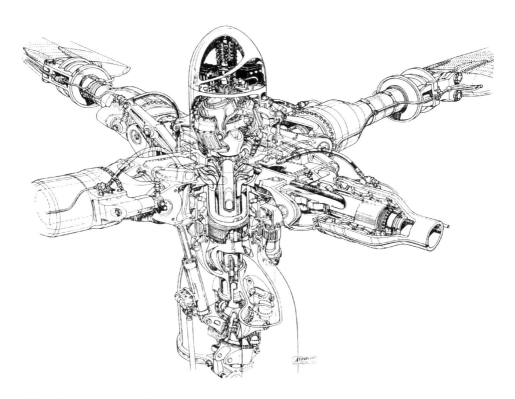

Blade and rotor head assembly. (Reproduced by kind permission from *Aeroplane*)

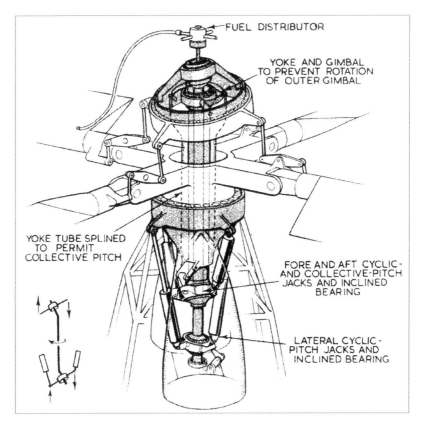

Arrangement of rotor head controls. (Reproduced by kind permission from *Flight International*)

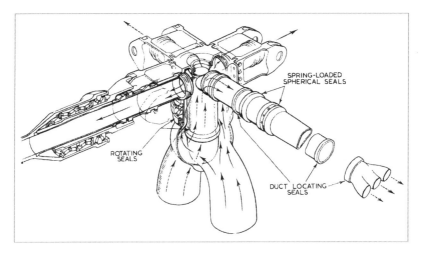

Air from the two auxiliary-compressors was separated to pass through concentric ducts in the assembly in order to provide air to diametrically opposite pairs of blades, thereby allowing sustained rotor power on a single engine. (Reproduced by kind permission from *Flight International*)

A low-voltage electrical supply through the rotor head ran via a slipring assembly mounted above the swash plate to four dual high-energy ignition units, situated in the dome, which formed the rotor hub. High-energy electrical power was then passed along the blades to the tip-jet igniters. A fuel supply also passed through the rotor head to the blades for the tip-jets. An accessory drive for the No.2 system hydraulic pump was also included to provide a separate system, driven from the rotor, to safeguard the control system in the event of a No.1 system failure.

Four stub arms were bolted to the head carrying the flapping hinges.

Rotor Blades

The rotor blade was built up of two main sections: a circular spar approximately 8ft/2.43m long, manufactured from forged stainless steel, detachable at its inner end from the feathering hinge lugs, and carrying at its outboard end the main portion of the blade. Lag hinges were not considered necessary because blade flapping angles in the cruise condition were small.

The main structure of the rotor blades was manufactured from stainless steel. Compressed air was ducted through three thin-walled stainless steel tubes to the jet units. The trailing edge fairings consisted of a number of floating light-alloy segments.

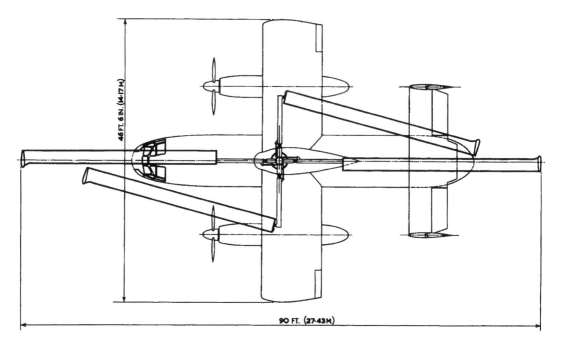

The proposed arrangement for blade folding. Two blades would be hydraulically folded to line up with two fore-and-aft blades.

The working section of the blade consisted of a stainless steel box section main spar, which formed the leading edge of the aerofoil section (NACA 0015). The trailing edge was manufactured from light alloy.

Air for the tip-jets was carried through three thin-walled stainless steel tubes. The jet units were secured at the outer end of the blade. Fuel and high-tension leads for jet ignition were carried down the leading edge.

Although not incorporated in the experimental flight test aircraft, it was the intention to incorporate electrical de-icing into production aircraft. It was also planned to provide power folding for the rotor, for which two blades would be aligned fore and aft, and the two lateral blades would then fold by aligning on the fore and aft axis.

Power plants

The Rotodyne was powered by two Napier Eland N.E.L.7 shaft turbine engines, each with a maximum continuous power rating of 3250shp.

The engine units were basically the same as those used for fixed-wing applications, but differed by the installation of a rear-end drive for the compressor, to supply air to the rotor jets.

The Eland had a single shaft carrying a three-stage turbine and a ten-stage axial flow compressor. The turbine was driven by six separate combustion chambers.

Drives for the propeller governor and fuel pump were taken from the compressor drive itself, with the result that a transmission failure between compressor and reduction gear would not affect engine speed control.

The engine air intake was protected against ice formation by the circulation of lubricating oil through the outer casing and the radial webs between the casing and the gearbox.

Auxiliary Compressor

The Eland engines installed in the Rotodyne had to perform two separate tasks. In cruising flight, the engines were called upon to perform as conventional turboprops, but, when operating in the helicopter regime, provision was made to supply compressed air to the tip-jets. This was accomplished by the addition of a rearward shaft extension to drive an auxiliary-compressor through a fluid clutch.

The unit took the form of an axial flow compressor capable of absorbing 80 per cent of the total engine power. Between them, the two compressor units could supply air at 45lb/sec (20kg/sec) at a pressure ratio of 4:1. The rate of flow out to the tip-jets was controlled by an arrangement of multiple flaps in the intake annulus, known colloquially as the 'umbrella valve', which was operated by movement of the collective pitch lever.

While operating in the helicopter regime, yaw control was accomplished by applying differential pitch to the propellers.

Propellers

The two large propellers were Rotol Type R146/4-40-6/1s, four blade variable pitch, with a diameter of 13ft/3.96m, and with a range from reverse pitch to fully feathered. Constant speeding of the propeller/engine combination was achieved by use of an engine fuel governing device, which allowed for the propeller pitch to be adjusted differentially at very low thrust to provide yaw control in the hover and low-speed condition.

Feathering was achieved by a conventional feathering unit, coupled to an anti-torque switch to ensure automatic feathering in the event of an engine failure.

The Tip-Jet Units

The tip-jet units were mounted tangentially on the blade tips. They were defined as pressure-jets, being distinctly different from ramjets, pulse-jets or small turbines. Air was supplied directly from the auxiliary-compressor, passing through the rotor head and along the blades, entering the combustion chamber from the side. There was, in fact, very little pressure loss due to friction, which was compensated for by a pressure gain through the rotating blade.

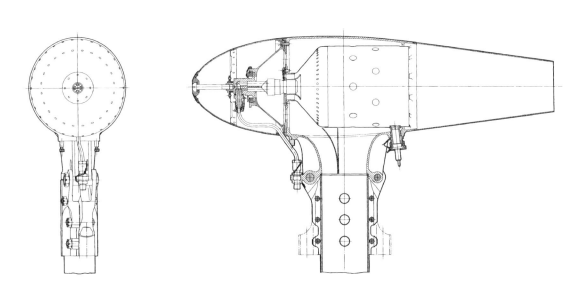

Achieving a satisfactory standard of even combustion from this side entry, converted to tangential thrust, was one of the most persistent problems which had to be solved during the tip-jet development.

The combustion chamber contained a liner manufactured from Nimonic 75. This liner was plunged with a pattern of holes designed to achieve an even Vortex pattern for efficient combustion.

The actual jet efflux cone, and later the silencer units, had to withstand temperatures up to 800°C, while subjected to centrifugal force as high as 350g, and the core flame temperature within the combustion chamber could reach 1,700-1,800°C.

Fuel was provided by a fuel regulator situated in the main rotor pylon, which metered fuel to the main rotor head, which then passed down the blades with CF (centrifugal force) providing the necessary pressure head for the conical Vortex sprayers situated at the head of the combustion chamber.

The development of the tip-jet units alone was one of the great achievements of the Rotodyne programme. Not only were the units robust and able to withstand the high stresses generated at the blade tips, but they performed with efficient combustion, while withstanding extreme temperatures, and proved to have reliable light-up and relight performance.

The tip-jets were deliciously simple in their design and function; there were in fact no moving parts, and they performed their function while creating low drag due to their small frontal area.

Control and Operation

Rotodyne had two regimes of flight. It could operate as a pure helicopter, relying upon the rotor for control, and power for forward flight, or, at a suitable time, it was possible to translate into an autogiro mode, whereby the rotor was no longer driven directly and propellers provided forward thrust.

The flight profile of the Rotodyne proceeded as follows:

After starting the engine, the auxiliary-compressor was engaged, passing air to the tip-jets. The rotor was then allowed to accelerate to light-up speed (approximately 100rpm). Fuel cocks were turned on and ignition selected, light-up generally followed in five to ten seconds. With the tip-jets burning successfully, the rotor was then accelerated up to the flight condition (approximately 140rpm).

Opposite page: The tip-jet units were elegant in their simplicity, consisting of only a combustion chamber, fuel supply/atomiser and igniter. Once light-up was achieved, combustion was self sustaining.

The aircraft was now ready to take off and operate in the helicopter regime:

- Rotor driven by tip-jets.
- Control in pitch, roll and hover positioning achieved by use of the cyclic pitch control.
- Lift provided by the rotor through the collective pitch control lever.
- Yaw control achieved by application of differential propeller pitch.

Once airborne the aircraft could achieve forward flight operating as a helicopter:

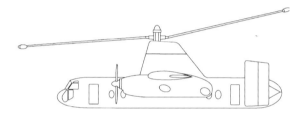

- Rotor powered by tip-jets.
- Forward flight achieved as a helicopter through the rotor by application of collective pitch and cyclic pitch.
- Cyclic pitch used to control the aircraft in pitch and roll.
- Yaw control achieved by application of differential propeller pitch, augmented by the aerodynamic rudders as speed increased.

The transfer from one flight regime to the other is known as the transition. This operation was developed to a simple cockpit drill, and was virtually imperceptible to the passengers.

While operating in forward flight, as a helicopter, the pilot accelerated, still climbing to his chosen transition speed in the range 90–110 knots. As speed increased, he reduced his tip-jet power down to the minimum, balancing power demand by increasing propeller pitch. Immediately before transition he stabilised rotor speed at about 140rpm, while maintaining a small nose-up attitude and setting propeller pitch to give a gentle rate of climb. At this point he moved a single lever, which cut the fuel flow to the tip-jets and declutched both compressors. Rotor power thereupon would fall to zero.

Over the following ten seconds or so, collective pitch would be reduced to about 3° and rotor speed allowed to fall slowly to the autorotation level, initially about 120rpm. During this period the pilot would maintain incidence by applying small corrections to elevator and cyclic pitch. The essential feature is that although a final small change in rotor power was made, all other changes, in particular fore-and-aft trim, remained smooth and continuous, and allowed the pilot plenty of time for any necessary control movement. It was possible for the transition to be reversed at any stage.

The climbing and accelerating flight path could be maintained with very little variation of fuselage attitude.

Forward flight in the Gyroplane regime (tip–jets OFF).

- Tip-jets shutdown and rotor established in autorotation
- Power for forward flight maintained through the propellers.
- Pitch and roll control achieved through cyclic pitch on the rotor and conventional aircraft controls.
- Yaw control maintained by use of rudders.

With the aircraft in this condition the total lift was evenly distributed between the rotor and the wings.

Transition back to helicopter flight was essentially a reversal of the procedure, reducing speed to 110 knots and engaging the auxiliary-compressor to provide air to the tip-jets, fuel and ignition was selected to achieve light–up.

Usually power for helicopter flight was re–established within four to five seconds.

Test Instrumentation

Instrumentation is the payload of any test vehicle or experimental aircraft. Throughout the entire ground and flight test programme the aircraft carried a comprehensive instrumentation fit capable of gathering vital data on all areas of interest or concern, covering handling and performance, power plant and aircraft systems functioning, structural integrity (including rotor head and blade stresses) and tip-jet performance.

'A good day at the office.' The forward part of the cabin was fitted out to carry the extensive instrumentation. Two or more observers (flight test engineers) were carried on all flights.

The forward area of the cabin was taken up by two large auto-observer panels, which recorded steady state parameters by means of 35mm cine cameras, controlled and monitored by the flight crew, backed up with the faithful knee-pad.

Dynamic measurements were gathered from multi-channel, continuous trace recorders.

The pilots' instruments were supplemented with aircraft attitude indication and blade droop stop proximity warnings.

There was an extensive strain gauge fit, with approximately 250 strain gauges recording blade and rotor head stresses, in addition to which there was a comprehensive coverage for the airframe structure. Strain gauge data was recorded using multi-channel galvanometer trace recorders. Accelerometers were also fitted to record vibration.

The recording of rotating parameters such as blade stresses and control movement at the rotor head was accomplished by means of a specially designed thirty-five-channel slip ring installation.

The quantity of data gathered on a single flight was vast, often amounting to some 300ft of 35mm cine film, all of which had to be analysed frame-by-frame, in addition to which there would be extensive trace recordings for stress and vibration.

All the Rotodyne work took place in an age before computers capable of reducing the workload were available; analysis of flight records was a labour intensive and time-consuming task, which was generally required with some urgency. It was a painstaking and somewhat arduous process, which was difficult to undertake with great enthusiasm, but nevertheless generally became the lot of the more diligent and competent members of the team. The VHF radio transmissions during test flights were recorded and backed up by a simple portable cockpit voice recorder.

The forward instrumentation control crew stations and instrumentation fit remained in place throughout the flight test programme. The normal flight crew consisted of two pilots and at least two flight test engineers (or flight test observers, as they were known at the time). There was also provision for additional crewmembers to be carried as required.

Early in 1959, the rear half of the fuselage was fully furnished with twenty seats and soundproofing, to full airline standards, allowing an opportunity for additional subjective experience and flight demonstration.

The Development of the Rotodyne Prototype

The Rotodyne prototype was designed and manufactured in Fairey's main factory at Hayes, Middlesex. The aircraft was then transported by road to the flight test facility based on White Waltham airfield.

At the end of the Second World War, the government of the time decided to develop Heathrow as London's main airport, thereby displacing the Fairey Aviation Company from its flight test airfield at Hounslow.

The final assembly and flight test operations were moved to White Waltham, where the offices and hangars once occupied by the Air Transport Auxiliary (ATA) had

The completed aircraft was transported to White Waltham in convoy, using public roads, during the early hours of the morning.

become available, and provided a ready-made home. From this time on, Fairey regularly transported completed airframes some twenty-five miles on public roads.

The Rotodyne, even with the wings and fuselage transported separately, was by far the largest load undertaken. The task was carried out during the quiet hours of the early morning, over a carefully planned route, and the aircraft was assembled in the newly erected large hangar which had been specially built for the Rotodyne programme.

White Waltham, in 1956, was a very busy place, already engaged in the assembly and flight clearance of Gannet anti-submarine aircraft coming off the production line, development of the airborne early warning version of the Gannet. The Ultra-Light helicopter programme was at the peak of its activity, with three development aircraft fully engaged on trials. The Jet Gyrodyne was still flying, engaged in the important task of perfecting and understanding the 'transition' process, and the management of the test programme for the record-breaking Fairey Delta 2. Supersonic test aircraft were also handled by the flight test department.

The Rotodyne prototype carried the military serial number XE521 throughout its flight programme, recognising its status as an experimental aircraft, built and financed to the requirements of the Ministry of Aviation.

The Rotodyne flew for the first time on 6 November 1957. The build standard for the initial flight was fairly rudimentary; the aircraft was left in its natural metal state,

The initial engine runs were carried out before final build was completed. The large hangar in the background was specially built to house the Rotodyne for the flight test programme.

Rotodyne pictured during its first flight on 7 November 1957. The undercarriage was fixed in the down position and heavily braced. Some engine panels were left of to ensure adequate cooling, and the upper fins were also removed.

unpainted. Apart from the serial number in black on the lower fin, the upper fins were left off, and the undercarriage was heavily braced to avoid the risk of resonance problems. Some sections of the engine cowlings were left off to ensure adequate cooling.

The test programme continued for over four years, during which time it completed 454 flights and a total duration of 154 hours.

The main object of the programme was to demonstrate that the revolutionary concept of a jet-driven compound helicopter was safe and reliable at all times, and that the transition process from helicopter to gyroplane mode could be safely accomplished with confidence.

During the first seventy flights, the aircraft was flown as a helicopter with the tip-jets driving the rotor. During this phase the speed was gradually increased to 130 knots. The first transition was accomplished in April 1958, and, during the flight programme, a total of 302 transitions were completed each way. Many of these transitions were carried out during the climb or in manoeuvres, including operations under IFR (Instrument Flight Rules) conditions.

Once the transition technique had been mastered, work then proceeded to extend the flight envelope in the autorotative regime. The forward speed capability was progressively increased until, on 5 January 1959, the Rotodyne set up a world speed record for convertiplanes, reaching 167 knots (307kph) over a 100km closed circuit. The Kamov Ka-22 twin-rotor compound helicopter later took the record when it exceeded 197 knots (365kph), in October 1961. Subsequent to this, the Rotodyne had been flown at level speeds as high as 180 knots, a considerable achievement when judged in relation to the 1953 design aim, which called for a cruise speed of 130 knots.

Most of the basic development was carried out during the first two years of the flight programme, by which time the operational concept was fully demonstrated together with a realistic flight envelope.

Flying generally took place operating from the Fairey Aviation test airfield at White Waltham. At first sight the flying rate does not appear to be very high, but this is well in keeping with the experimental nature of the aircraft, and the standard achieved from the 250 flights carried out during this basic development phase would indicate that very efficient use was being made of the flying time.

With any flight test programme it is a popular misconception that the flying rate is an indication of progress. Properly planned flight programmes include provision for adequate downtime, to allow for analysis and modification, but it also has to be accepted that there may be long periods when the weather makes it impossible to gather high-quality data.

In June 1959 the Rotodyne flew from London airport to the Allée Verte Heliport, Brussels, and then on to the Issy Heliport in Paris. The underlying purpose of this exercise was to attend the 23rd Aeronautical Salon at Le Bourget, but it was also recognised as an opportunity to demonstrate the advantages of VTOL operations. The Rotodyne accomplished this journey in fifty-eight minutes, which was half the time achievable by conventional helicopter, and the two-stage journey would not be achievable in the same time by a fixed-wing airliner, bearing in mind the ground time involved at each of the airfields.

The achievement of the speed record and the completion of the European flight were defining moments in the Rotodyne programme. The two events gave a clear indication that the concept could fulfil its promise.

Although the basic development programme continued, space was found to insert specific exercises associated with the basic role as a civil airliner, and for further development as a large transport helicopter with both civil and military applications.

One such exercise involved the transportation and positioning of a prefabricated bridge, measuring 103ft/31.4m. During this demonstration the bridge was transported five miles (8km) across country, and placed accurately across a river. On other occasions underslung loads of up to 8,000lb/3,630kg were carried.

Rotodyne was demonstrated at the Society of British Aircraft Constructors show at Farnborough in September 1959. For this occasion the rear section of the fuselage was fully furnished to airline standard, and part of the demonstration included the carriage of thirty nurses.

Prior to the Farnborough exercise, in order to complete the furnishing of the rear section, and to install modifications arising from the flight test work carried out during the first phase of the programme, the aircraft was flown into the Hayes factory, which was situated in a built-up part of suburban London.

A flight into Battersea Heliport, on the river Thames, not far from the Houses of Parliament, was carried out, during which comprehensive noise measurements were gathered. The Battersea helipad measured only 125ft x 55ft/38m x 16m.

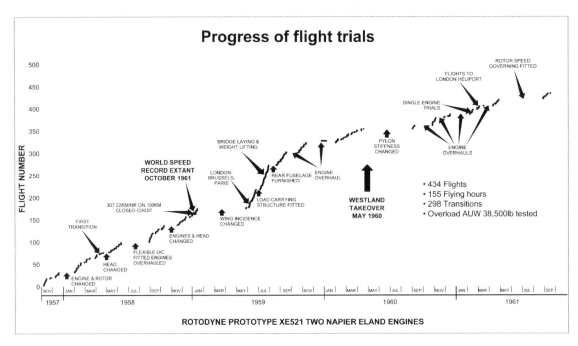

Diagram showing the progress of the flight trials over the whole programme. All major events are annotated.

Several flights were made from RAE Bedford and RAF Benson, to assess baulked landings and single-engine run-on landings. Here they demonstrated one of the claimed safety features of the Rotodyne: that in normal flight it was already established in autorotation, and was consequently much more manageable in an emergency situation.

The rationalisation of the British aircraft industry in 1960 had a profound effect on the Rotodyne programme; with both companies being preoccupied with commercial issues, progress temporarily slowed.

When official support was finally withdrawn in 1962, the Rotodyne prototype was considered to have reached a high level of maturity. The design, mock-up and preliminary rig testing for the larger Tyne-powered production aircraft was well in advance.

The Tip-Jet Test Facility

The use of tip-jets as a primary drive system called for a very specialised test facility. Even in the early stages it was fully appreciated that a considerable amount of noise would be generated, and that the demands of a busy test programme would mean operating outside the normal working day on occasions.

The single-blade spinning rig, which was part of the White Waltham test facility and played a vital role in the test programme.

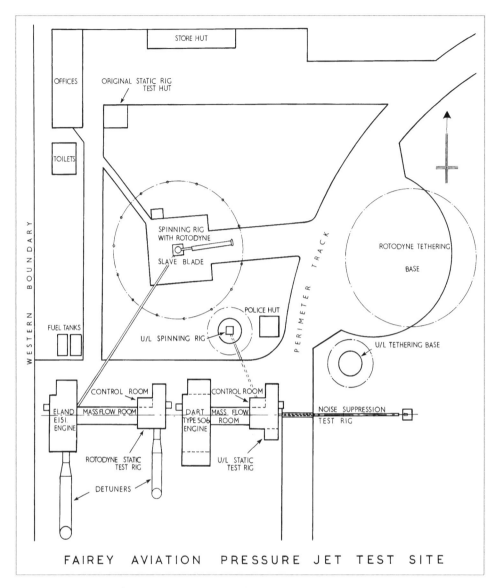

STORE HUT

OFFICES

ORIGINAL STATIC RIG
TEST HUT

TOILETS

SPINNING RIG
WITH ROTODYNE

SLAVE BLADE

ROTODYNE TETHERING

BASE

POLICE HUT

FUEL TANKS

U/L SPINNING RIG

U/L TETHERING BASE

CONTROL ROOM

CONTROL ROOM

ELAND
E151
ENGINE

MASS FLOW ROOM

DART
TYPE 506
ENGINE

MASS FLOW
ROOM

NOISE SUPPRESSION
TEST RIG

ROTODYNE STATIC
TEST RIG

U/L STATIC
TEST RIG

DETUNERS

WESTERN BOUNDARY

PERIMETER TRACK

FAIREY   AVIATION   PRESSURE   JET   TEST   SITE

A site plan showing the full extent of the tip-jet test facility at White Waltham.

The chosen site for this work was at the company's airfield and flight test establishment at White Waltham, placing the compound in the north-west corner of the airfield, well clear of residential areas, and care was taken to place it well away from the company's own office area.

When first built in the 1950s, the site consisted primarily of a single test cell for which air was supplied by a single Rolls-Royce Dart engine, specially modified for the purpose. As time progressed the facility was enlarged to undertake testing on Jet-Gyrodyne and Ultra-Light helicopter, including arrangements to run a spinning facility.

A Rotodyne tip-jet unit on test in one of the cells at White Waltham. The installation was comprehensively fitted with instrumentation, and played a key role in the development programme.

By the time the Rotodyne programme came into line, the site was one of the most comprehensive test facilities of its kind in Europe, comprising of two cells for testing the static performance of the pressure-jet units, a spinning rig to test jet units on a slave blade, and a fixed outdoor static rig for noise tests and silencer development.

The original Dart installation was subsequently replaced by twin Rolls-Royce Avon engines, modified to provide the necessary flow of air.

A well-appointed workshop was available, capable of fabricating sophisticated jet unit components including combustion liners and silencers, working with the specialised materials involved (i.e. Nimonic alloy and stainless steel).

The proximity of these facilities to the main flight test establishment resulted in a well-integrated response to flight test problems, keeping delays to a minimum.

The main aircraft tie-down facility for tethered ground running and resonance testing was also situated adjacent to the test site.

Main Rotor Running Rig at Boscombe Down

It was decided quite early in the planning stage of the programme that the introduction of a full-scale main rotor running rig would be of great value, and that this should be ready to commence testing well in advance of the first flight.

Some consideration was given regarding the location of such a facility, and the Ministry of Supply agreed to site the rig at the Aircraft and Armament Experimental Establishment (A&AEE) on the airfield at Boscombe Down, Wiltshire.

The rig was a complete representation of the rotor system, power plants and controls with all the key components in their correct physical relationship to the rotor, and it

The main and rotor running rig was assembled at Hayes before dispatch for re-assembly at Boscombe Down.

was also decided that the facility should be operated and serviced in the same fashion as an aircraft, in order that flight–standard components could be fitted and run without compromising serviceability.

The instrumentation included provision for main rotor strain gauge measurements and tip-jet performance. The control cabin was laid out to represent the aircraft where possible, to help familiarise the pilots in advance of the flight programme.

Once the design was assembled in the factory at Hayes, the components were transported from the factory at Hayes to Boscombe Down, and the final construction of the rig accomplished. The whole installation was housed within its own compound

The rotor and power plant running rig in situ at Boscombe Down. The rig was capable of running flight standard components and engines with full validation. Such rigs are now commonplace, but at that time they represented a very innovative approach.

and encircled by a high earth bank sited well away from the main offices so that it would cause minimum disturbance.

Initial engine runs took place in April 1957, and the build standard was progressively improved until, by the following August, a fully representative run with twin engines and four rotor blades, with full instrumentation, was possible. The first task carried out by the rig was to run the flight engines and aircraft blades, before the assembly to the aircraft itself. A total of fifty hours rotor running was accomplished during this phase, giving confidence regarding the maturity of the whole power and rotor system sufficient to commence the programme.

During the pre-flight running it was possible to take measurements of rotor power and blade stresses, propeller strain gauge measurements, control functions and assessment of lubrication and seals, with sufficient time to incorporate modifications to the system on the aircraft in advance of its first flight.

The operation of the rig during this phase was predominantly in the hands of the pilots, in order to ensure that they were thoroughly familiar with the operation of the system.

The rig remained in continuous use until the programme was finally terminated in 1962. Its value to the project cannot be overstated. Pre-flight running at Boscombe Down supported all phases of the flight test programme.

The facility was also used for main rotor blade stress data gathering, tip-jet and silencer development and aircraft systems support.

Mathematical Modelling for Fairey Rotodyne

It is easy to forget that during the period that the Rotodyne was designed, the calculating aids available to engineers and designers were comparatively simple by modern standards. The basic tool being the faithful slide rule – every engineer and technician had his own!

For the more elaborate or critical circulations, a range of electro-mechanical calculating machines were available. These could add, subtract, multiply and divide, and with a little skill the square root was achievable, all to a fair level of accuracy. The main complaint was that they were incredibly noisy and expensive, when one bears in mind that their whole repertoire can now be achieved with the simple hand calculator, and in silence.

The Fairey Company was among the first to recognise the potential of the computer when, in 1960, they installed an Elliot 803 at Hayes to support the range of very advanced design tasks with which they were involved, namely Gannet, Fairey Delta FD-2, Ultra-light and Rotodyne.

The Elliott 803 was typical of its time, housed in several large cabinets in an air-conditioned room drawing about 3.5kw. Data input was done using a teleprinter and high-speed paper tape reader.

The operating speed, memory and capacity was a fraction of that now commonplace with home computers, but even so it represented a significant advance in the calculating power available, and, at a cost of £29,000, bears testament to the importance the Fairey Company placed on sound basic design.

In the mid-1950s, the Dynamics Department was set up at Hayes as part of the Technical Office, the purpose of which was to mathematically model the dynamic behaviour of the Fairey Rotodyne in four main areas. These were:

1. Prediction of the rotor blade natural frequencies and mode shapes in flap, lag and torsion.
2. Prediction of the response of the complete rotor system in the plane of rotation due to non-simultaneous light-up of the tip-jets, leading to lag plane oscillations of individual blades.

3. Minimisation of the forced response of the airframe due to rotor system vibratory forcing at four-per-rev frequency. The airframe was represented as an assembly of beams of defined stiffness, with point masses positioned at the beam junctions as required. It was fully realised that confidence could not be placed in the absolute values of predicted natural frequencies, but the method was valuable in indicating the trends of changes in natural frequencies with changes in structural stiffness in various regions of the airframe. The results from this analysis guided the design change consisting of the introduction of pitching flexibility into the rotor pylon, which significantly reduced the four-per-rev frequency vibration in flight.

4. Prediction of ground resonance behaviour in order to provide design guidance in the areas of undercarriage stiffness and damping characteristics, and rotor blade lag plane stiffness and damping requirements. It was considered that a fundamental analysis was required in order to gain basic insight into the problem, and also to avoid the approximation that would have to be made in order to apply the Coleman criteria for avoidance of instability. Since the application of the ground resonance theory indicated that ground resonance would occur within the rotor speed range during ground operation, a physical ground resonance model was designed, built and tested, which confirmed the predicted instability. This established confidence in the use of the mathematical model to guide the design modifications to the undercarriage characteristics and the rotor lag plane dynamics, to completely eliminate any tendency to ground resonance throughout the full range of ground operating conditions.

It is believed that the mathematical approaches that were developed for the four problem areas described above were unique in the industry at that time, and, in fact, formed the basis for further developments in analytical techniques, which were successfully applied to later designs of helicopters worldwide.

Ground Resonance

Ground resonance is a problem that can occur in all helicopters. It is such an important issue that some explanation of the phenomenon is necessary.

An articulated main rotor allows the blade to lead and lag in its own plane. This is necessary to alleviate the rotor hub components of Coriolis forcing due to the blade flapping motion. The existence of blade flapping motion gives rise to the possibility of a resonant condition. If the blades lag in phase, the centre of gravity of the rotor system remains on the axis of rotation, but non-in-phase motions of blades will cause the rotor system centre of gravity to move off the axis of rotation, and a type of stirring motion can be set up.

The undercarriage contains shock absorbers and dampers, and the aircraft will therefore have natural frequencies governed by the undercarriage and fuselage.

Consequently, any non-in-phase lag motion of the blades will cause a movement of the rotor centre of gravity off the axis of rotation, and the fuselage and its undercarriage will be subjected to an oscillatory force.

If this force is at a frequency close to that of the fuselage/undercarriage mode, then a dangerous resonant condition is a possibility.

The offset centre of gravity will trigger a rocking motion of the fuselage on its undercarriage. This will cause a translation motion (usually in a lateral direction) of the rotor hub, which can then drive the blade lagging motion.

By this means, a divergent situation can arise, which typically can result in severe damage, if not a complete break-up of the helicopter. In extreme cases ground resonance can destroy the helicopter in a matter of seconds.

A feature of the Rotodyne was its low damping in the lag plane of the rotor, and this, together with the design problems associated with the retracting undercarriage, required a special effort to overcome ground resonance.

It was decided at quite an early stage in the programme to build a dynamic model to investigate resonance issues. The model was built to a 1:15 scale (rotor diameter = 6ft/1.83m), and was constructed to represent all degrees of freedom of the aircraft on its undercarriage, and of the rotor. Mathematical analysis and model tests revealed that

This dynamic model was a scale representation of the undercarriage, airframe and rotor. It was used to predict resonant problems in advance of full-scale testing. Several problem areas were detected, and solutions found, in advance of full-scale running, using this facility.

Tests were carried out to confirm that the aircraft was free of ground resonance problems using a specially prepared facility where the new aircraft could be ground-run, standing free. Cables were attached at rotor head level, which could be tensioned hydraulically, to tether the aircraft in the event of an emergency.

the original undercarriage incurred two main narrow regions of instability near the maximum take-off rotor rpm. Accordingly, it was decided to undertake the first flight with the undercarriage stiffened by a bracing, which moved the resonance regions above normal rotor rpm, but imposed a vertical touch-down velocity limit which called for additional care on landing, although it was well within piloting capability.

Before undertaking the first flight, tests were made whereby the airframe was shaken at the top of the pylon using hydraulic jacks to apply the appropriate forces at a range of frequencies. The impedance testing included an assessment of airborne conditions, with the aircraft suspended from a crane.

Ground resonance testing was undertaken on a specially prepared running site adjacent to the tip-jet testing facility. This included an arrangement to restrain the aircraft with three cables situated at 120° to each other; these were attached at the top of the pylon close to the rotor head, and passed over supporting struts to hydraulic jacks situated outside the rotor diameter.

Aircraft running was undertaken with the cables untensioned, allowing the aircraft freedom of movement. If, during the run, instrumentation, or even direct observation, indicated a problem, the ground controller could tension the cables hydraulically, thereby clamping the aircraft.

Ground resonance tests were undertaken in this fashion prior to first flight, and subsequently before flying commenced with a fully retracting undercarriage.

Shake tests were carried out with the aircraft suspended from a crane through a soft air spring. Forces at various frequencies were applied using hydraulic jacks, while measuring the displacements of the structure.

Difficulty was experienced designing a retracting undercarriage with sufficient stiffness to move the natural frequency above the rotor rpm range, so a very soft undercarriage was designed.

This proved to be quite satisfactory because although there were regions of instability at about 115–125rpm, these did not cause trouble since the rate of divergence was slow. This soft undercarriage had rubber bobbins in the side, and drag struts which allowed the aircraft to be operated normally, except that prolonged running in the 115–125rpm range had to be avoided.

The original rubber bobbins had a rather short linear range, which imposed a limit on propeller pitch application on the ground, so a redesign was undertaken which extended the linear range and removed this limitation. It was considered that this solution would not be suitable for the operational aircraft, since rubber tends to change its characteristics with age. This could cause regions of instability to move towards the rotor running range.

It was considered that the regions of instability could be completely eliminated by the introduction of lag plane dampers on the rotor. Theoretical analysis and tests on the dynamic model confirmed this.

The damper installation was fitted and tested on the rig, and subsequently on the aircraft, with satisfactory results.

The Rotodyne main undercarriage leg. The fore, aft and lateral damper installations are clearly visible.

Towards the end of the programme, lag plane dampers were fitted to the rotor to reduce the effect of rotor inputs. These proved to be effective.

The Transition Process

The Rotodyne was a compound helicopter. This means that for take-off, landing and low-speed flight the aircraft flew as a helicopter, with the rotor powered by pressure jets at the blade tips, providing lift, thrust and control. For high-speed cruising flight the Rotodyne could operate as a gyroplane, the rotor then being unpowered and free to autorotate.

The rotor provided approximately 40 per cent lift in the gyroplane state, the remainder being provided by the wing, while thrust was provided by forward-facing propellers. The transfer from one flight regime to the other is known as the transition. This operation was developed to a simple cockpit drill and was virtually imperceptible to the passengers.

After climbing vertically to about 200ft/60m, the pilot accelerated, still climbing to his chosen transition speed in the range of 90–110 knots. As speed increased he reduced his tip-jet power down to the minimum, balancing power demand by increasing propeller pitch. Immediately before transition he would stabilise rotor speed at about 140rpm, hold a small nose-up attitude, and set propeller pitch to give a gentle rate of climb. At this point he would move a single lever, which cut the fuel flow to the tip-jets, and declutch both compressors. Rotor power thereupon fell to zero.

Over the following ten seconds or so, collective pitch was reduced to about 3° and rotor speed fell slowly to the autorotation level, initially about 120rpm. During this period the pilot maintained incidence by applying small corrections to elevator and cyclic pitch. The essential feature is that although a final small change in rotor power was made, all other changes, in particular fore-and-aft trim, remained smooth and continuous and allowed the pilot plenty of time for any necessary control movement, while leaving the optionfor the the transition to be reversed at any stage. The climbing, accelerating flight path could be maintained with very little variation of fuselage attitude.

As the test programme progressed, confidence was gained, and on many take-offs the jets were extinguished seventy seconds after lift-off, and on landing the light-up was often delayed until a mere thirty seconds before touch-down. During the flight test programme over 300 transitions were made each way, many of which were conducted in gentle manoeuvres. Several transitions were completed in heavy rain and severe turbulence, and in IFR conditions with the cloud base as low as 100ft/30m, with visibility restricted to 300ft/90m.

Aerodynamics

The Fairey Aviation Company was the first in Britain to install its own wind tunnel. This was housed in a stately building, which presented part of the frontage of the Hayes factory and was built in 1938. The wind tunnel was of the closed-circuit type, with the working section 12ft/3.6m wide by 10ft/3m high.

By the mid-1950s the aircraft speeds achievable were such that the Hayes tunnel was reaching its limitations, it was, however, ideally suited for helicopter applications.

The 1:15th scale model installed in the Hayes wind tunnel showing the electrically driven rotor, which was held in aerodynamic contact only. This model was mainly used to assess the rotor airframe relationship.

Extensive use of the wind tunnel was made during the Rotodyne programme, amounting to well over 1,000 hours. Two wind tunnel models were made. The largest was made to a 1:6 scale, giving a wingspan of 9ft/2.75m, which was the largest acceptable size for the wind tunnel working section. This model was used to assess slipstream measurements, directional stability and drag reduction. The smaller model was made to a 1:15 scale, giving a wingspan of 3.1ft/1m, and was provided with a rotor (rotor diameter = 6ft/1.8m). The rotor was driven separately and maintained in aerodynamic contact only.

This model was used to assess airframe rotor relationship, rotor blade flapping in all modes of flight, and effect of rotor downwash.

An active wind tunnel programme was maintained throughout the flight development phase, and played an important part in the decision-making process resolving important issues such as wing incidence, fin arrangement and drag reduction.

During the early test flights with the aircraft operating as a helicopter at comparatively low speeds (below 40 knots/74kph), the control through the rotor was found to be extremely good. Directional control at low speeds, which relied on differential propeller pitch, was found to be rather sluggish, but was considered adequate.

In the aircraft's original build configuration, the upper fins were set at a dihedral angle of 60°, with the intention of achieving good directional stability and an increased

The fins in their original configuration, with 60° dihedral, which resulted in poor stability in roll and yaw.

longitudinal stability. Wind tunnel results and flight test experience indicated that the overall dihedral effect was too high. It was eventually appreciated that this effect came largely from the fins and the design was modified so that the fins were raised to a vertical position for flight, thus eliminating the worst lateral coupling effects.

It should be noted that the fins were set in a horizontal position prior to take-off, until the rotor was running up to speed, to avoid the danger of structural contact due to a blade flapping motion. They were raised to the vertical 'flight' position once the rotor was up to speed, prior to lift off, and remained so throughout the flight, until after landing when they were lowered to the horizontal position before the rotor was allowed to run down. The fin modifications were incorporated during the first major lay-up in mid-1958. As the programme progressed, it was noted that directional stability was still marginal, and so, during a major lay-up in 1960, a third fin was added with satisfactory results.

As the speed was increased beyond the original design speed of 130 knots/240kph, it was found that control was becoming marginal, and, in particular, rolling power was low and lateral control became inadequate in high sideslip.

Setting the fins to the vertical position for flight brought about immediate improvements in stability, which was improved even further by the introduction of a third fin.

In the original design control in roll was achieved through the rotor with lateral-cyclic, and the only aerodynamic control in roll was the addition of a small trim tab on the port wing. Eventually, however, a full set of ailerons was installed with the result that satisfactory rolling characteristics and control were achieved.

The relationship between the wing and the rotor through the speed range in the two regimes of flight (helicopter and gyroplane) had to be investigated. When operating as a helicopter all lift came from the rotor powered by the tip-jets. As speed increased a small contribution of lift came from the fuselage and wing. The resultant effect was to increase blade flapping, which would have an ongoing effect on fatigue life. The rotor speed in the helicopter regime was 140rpm. Similarly, once in the gyroplane regime, with lower rotor speed and high forward speed, lift was now evenly divided between the wing and the rotor. The rotor speed for the gyroplane condition was set at a value of 120rpm.

As the programme progressed, the allowable forward speed was increased to 150 knots/278kph, and the combined effect of wing incidence and the fitting of silencers had the effect of increasing the backward mechanical flapping of the rotor, which indicated a need to reduce wing incidence.

The wing incidence was reduced from 4° to zero, during a major lay-up early in 1959, prior to the London-Brussels-Paris flight and the Paris Show. This had an immediate effect, improving longitudinal control positions in high-speed cruise, with the result that backward flapping of the blades was reduced, thereby improving the fatigue situation and allowing better control margins for manoeuvre.

A considerable amount of work was carried out using the 1:6 scale wind tunnel model to assess airframe drag at high speeds. The basic airframe contributed approximately one-sixth of the total drag. The need for increased tail stiffening resulted in the introduction of large round struts, which resulted in a disproportionate increase in drag. Faired struts subsequently replaced these. The bifurcated jet pipes were also found to be a source of drag. For subsequent designs it was intended to incorporate the single-sided jet pipe, flush mounted and exhausting outboard.

Wind tunnel tests showed that the rotor head fairing was indeed a source of high drag, so work was put in hand to produce fairings for the rotor stub arms. Rotor profile drag constituted a large proportion of the total drag.

Performance

The two engines installed in the prototype Rotodyne were Napier Eland N.E.L.3s, which had a maximum power rating (at sea level) of 2,800shp. Each engine was arranged to drive an auxiliary compressor, connected through a clutch, to provide air for four Fairey pressure-jet units.

The engine planned for the proposed production of forty-seat aircraft was the Napier Eland N.E.L.7, which had a maximum power rating (at sea level) of 3,250shp, and a one hour rating (at sea level) of 2,900shp.

The maximum permitted forward speed for the prototype was laid down at 150 knots/ 278kph. Provision was made for clearance to exceed this for specific exercises (e.g. to set speed records).

It was intended that the production aircraft would have a cruising speed of 160 knots/ 296kph. It should be noted that the original British European Airways requirement called for a speed of 135 knots/250.1kph.

In April 1957, Fairey issued a weights and performance appendix (ref: FAC-TH 1034), from which the following data could be derived:

- Range: the stage distance with forty passengers was to be 250 nautical miles/ 463km.
- The hover ceiling (out of ground effect) with two engines, providing maximum tip-jet power, was to be 10,500ft/3,200m (ISA).
- The vertical rate of climb, with two engines providing maximum tip-jet power, was to be 2,500ft/762m per minute (at sea level).

- The rate of climb with a gyroplane regime, with two engines running at the one-hour rating, was to be 2,000ft/609m per minute (ISA), at sea level, reducing to 1,100ft/305m per minute at 10,000ft.
- In tip-jet powered flight (helicopter regime), operating with a single engine, one-hour rating, the aircraft would be expected to be capable of a 150ft/45m per minute rate of climb, at all take-off altitudes and temperatures at which the aircraft will operate.
- In autorotational flight (gyroplane regime), operating with a single engine, one-hour rating, the aircraft would be expected to be capable of a 150ft/45m per minute rate of climb, at weights below maximum, or at moderate temperatures.

The above conditions were laid down for an aircraft operating with an all-up weight at take-off of 35,000lb/1,588kg, with fuel allowances laid by SBAC:

- Three minutes at maximum tip-jet power for take-off and landing.
- Twenty minutes standoff in gyroplane regime.
- 1.5 per cent allowance on fuel used.
- 5 per cent allowance on fuel carried.

Work carried out with XE521, which included the London–Brussels–Paris flight, and the single-engine landings demonstrations, all with the lower-powered N.E.L.3 engines, gave confidence that the desired performance criteria could be met.

Vibration

The control of vibration has always been one of the major preoccupations for the helicopter designer. In an elastic system subjected to periodic forces, large amplitudes of vibration can result from quite small forces – if the forcing frequency is in the neighbourhood of the natural frequency of the elastic system, and if the damping of the system is small.

In the case of a rotorcraft the predominant forcing frequency is the product of rotor speed and the number of blades. The mathematical analysis carried out in advance of the Rotodyne flight programme predicted that three modes or resonance regions would occur within or near the rotor running range.

From the outset pilots experienced very heavy vibration during the flare out to hover in helicopter mode, where the rotor speed was in the region of 140rpm. This was very apparent through the rudder pedals, so much so that it was extremely difficult for the pilots to hold their feet in place during this very critical phase of flight, and, of course, it was very uncomfortable for the crew and passengers.

Excessive vibration was also evident in the gyroplane mode, when the rotor speed was at approximately 120rpm, becoming very apparent as forward speed was increased.

A considerable amount of flying was devoted to vibration data gathering. This included one experiment where a large strut was introduced between the top of the pylon and the tail, with the empennage (tailplane and fins) being removed. Analysis of this experiment and the results gathered from basic data indicated that the vibration occurring during high-speed flight could be reduced to acceptable levels by reducing the stiffness of the pylon, and that the vibration occurring during transition to hover could be substantially improved by the introduction of tailplane dampers. The main rotor pylon structure was, therefore, modified to incorporate small dampers in the rear supports, allowing a small degree of movement in pitch.

The maintenance of main rotor tracking, whereby the tip paths of all blades coincide, is a common problem encountered by all helicopters. Keeping rotor blades in track is accepted as the primary means of keeping basic vibration down to an acceptable level.

The methods used to assess rotor track during the 1960s were not sophisticated, and difficult to apply to a large helicopter such as the Rotodyne where the blade tips where 22ft/6.7m above the ground. In any case it was desirable and more representative to be able to assess a tracking issue in flight and through the speed range.

Towards the end of the programme tracking was assessed using an electronic tracker, which measured the height of the blade as it passed over a sensor situated on the rear fuselage. Adjustments applied on the basis of data acquired using this equipment resulted in a considerable improvement.

As the flight programme progressed, vibration levels progressively improved, resulting in a very acceptable ride, considered by most passengers to be comparable with that of any of the contemporary turbo-prop airliners.

Noise

Noise was a major preoccupation throughout the Rotodyne programme. From a subjective viewpoint, no one could deny that the Rotodyne was very noisy, and a considerable amount of effort was expended trying to establish criteria which would satisfy critics, but this proved to be extremely difficult.

A large amount of time and money was spent on silencer development, more than forty silencer efflux patterns were made and tested on the White Waltham rigs, in addition to which the company maintained high-level representation of all discussion groups whose work might lead to producing acceptable noise levels.

Even though half a century has elapsed since the Rotodyne first flew, it is still generally considered that the main reason for its failure was the noise problem. With this in mind it is worth considering this at length.

The Helicopter Noise Problem

The Ministry of Aviation, which was responsible for legislation at the time, produced a report concerning helicopter noise, and this was even before the Rotodyne was causing some concern. The content of this report can be summarised as follows:

Units and Standards:

There is considerable complexity in the choice of units in which objective measurement of noise should be expressed to give a meaningful indication. For the purposes of this report it is considered best and simplest to give numerical information in terms of internationally agreed units of loudness (phons), the loudness levels being computed by S.S. Stevens. An increase (or decrease) of ten phons doubles (or halves) the loudness.

Comparative loudness levels:

Aircraft over central London	95 phons
Traffic noise in central London (inc. passing buses)	95 phons
Quiet back street with little or no traffic	70–75 phons
Outside traffic (from indoors)	65–75 phons
Inside underground train (Metro)	100 phons
London Underground station platform	103 phons
IPod/MP3 player set to 90 per cent volume	>85 phons
Cinema during a high noise level sequence	110 phons

In general it was considered that noise levels indoors would be reduced by approximately twenty phons if the windows were closed. In office conditions, perceived noise levels were generally down by a further five to ten phons for those working above the third floor.

Subjective rating for noises affecting voice communication:

Loudness level (Phons)	Acceptability	Voice communication
100	intolerable	voice very loud at 1ft
90	unpleasantly noisy voice very loud at 2ft	voice raised at 1ft
80	noisy	normal voice at 2ft voice raised at 4ft voice very loud at 6ft
70	moderately noisy	natural voice levels
50	quiet to very quiet	

Noise levels generated by contemporary helicopters (*c.*1960):

Type	Operation	Measuring station	Loudness
Widgeon	Take-off	500ft from pad, under flight path	110 phons
	Landing	500ft from pad, under flight path	100 phons
	Cruise	1000ft under flight path	86 phons
Whirlwind	Take-off	500ft from pad, under flight path	103 phons
	Landing	500ft from pad, under flight path	103 phons
	Cruise	1000ft under flight path	90 phons
Wessex	Take-off	500ft from pad, under flight path	104 phons
	Landing	500ft from pad, under flight path	104 phons
	Cruise	1000ft under flight path	88 phons
Vertol	Take-off	500ft from pad, under flight path	90 phons
	Landing	500ft from pad, under flight path	109 phons
	Cruise	1000ft under flight path	78 phons
Rotodyne	Take-off	500ft from pad, under flight path	109 phons
	Landing	500ft from pad, under flight path	115 phons
	Cruise	1000ft under flight path	96 phons

Rotodyne Noise

The noise debate ran continuously throughout the Rotodyne programme; it was clear that British European Airways, who were the lead customer at this time, were very concerned about this issue. Whenever the Rotodyne made a public appearance that involved operation as a helicopter, tip-jets burning, the reaction was always the same: 'It is very noisy!'

The noise issue was almost entirely concerned with the tip-jets. Once the aircraft was operating as a gyroplane, it was indistinguishable from any turboprop airliner of similar size. The basic noise level of Rotodyne, operating in clear air with plain jets, generated a noise level in excess of 97db at take-off, measured 500ft from the take-off point at the moment of lift-off. The perceived noise level inside buildings was estimated to be 80db. This can be compared with the levels of a number of common sources previously shown.

Rotodyne Noise and Silencer Development

It was well understood from the outset that the noise issue would remain one of the main problems to be overcome. As early as 1956 a programme to determine the most effective silencer design commenced, the work centred upon the assessment of a range of orifice profiles for comparative tests.

Over forty nozzle configurations were tested using the static noise rig; these achieved a wide variation in results, and some regardless of the effect were considered to be impractical.

In the course of the noise test work it was found that pressure ratio and fuel/air ratio influenced noise from the jet solely due to their effect on jet velocity.

The environment in which the silencers would have to operate was very severe indeed, temperatures at the core at jet efflux could be as high as 1,800°C, and the tip-jet units could be subjected to a centrifugal force of 350g.

Only a few of the nozzles tested on the static rig were developed to an aircraft configuration for tests on the spinning rig, and of these the preferred option was a seven-lobe silencer which became known as the Type 8c. The '8c' silencers achieved an attenuation of 7db.

The design of the 8c silencer resulted in an efflux shape, which took the form of the seven-pointed star mounted in an annulus. The intention was to direct and to accelerate the airflow so that the external air met the high-velocity efflux as a parallel flow with minimal disturbance.

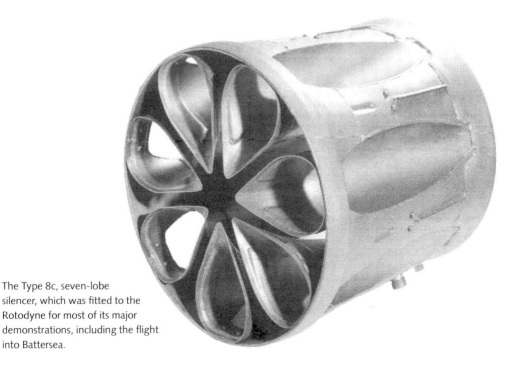

The Type 8c, seven-lobe silencer, which was fitted to the Rotodyne for most of its major demonstrations, including the flight into Battersea.

The 100km Closed-Circuit Speed Record

By the end of 1958, Fairey were confident that the Rotodyne had reached a high level of maturity, having achieved the main points of the required flight envelope. It was therefore decided that a public demonstration of the Rotodyne's potential would be beneficial.

An application was made to the Federation Aeronautique International (FAI) to recognise the new category of rotorcraft, the convertiplane, and to agree that the Rotodyne should attempt to establish a world speed record for the class.

It was decided to undertake a record over a 100km closed-circuit course, in preference to the 15km straight-line dash normally used to establish absolute speed records.

An even more important decision was that the attempt should not exceed one hour of continuous power rating for the Napier Eland plants. This, it was felt, would enable a record to be achieved under conditions in keeping with the commercial nature of the aircraft, and from a sales viewpoint the task would provide a far more convincing demonstration of the Rotodyne's potential.

The course was planned between White Waltham and Hungerford, making it possible to start and finish at Fairey's operating base. Provision was made for a wide 180° turn at Hungerford, laid out to overfly three checkpoints, allowing the aircraft to make the manoeuvre without losing speed. The actual course, when surveyed, measured 100.6km.

Weather conditions at the time of the record attempt were very good, with no more than 3 knots of wind blowing up and down the course at ground-level. The record run was carried out at fairly low level (650–750ft), mainly to assist the crew in identifying vital landmarks. It was important that the aircraft passed the finishing line at a higher altitude than at the start, as finishing below 650ft would mean disqualification.

The flight was carried out on 5 January 1959, and established a new speed record for rotorcraft at 190.9mph/307kph, representing an increase of 49mph/78.8kph over the existing 100km record, and 29mph/46.7kph faster than the then current absolute speed record for rotorcraft.

London–Brussels–Paris and the Paris Airshow at Le Bourget, June 1959

On 16 June 1959, the Rotodyne left Heathrow, in London, en-route to Paris, to take part in the 23rd Aeronautical Salon at Le Bourget. It was an important occasion in that it was the first time the Rotodyne had been taken outside the United Kingdom.

Having cleared customs at Heathrow, the Rotodyne took off and flew via Dover to Brussels, touching down at Allee Verte Heliport, situated in the heart of the city of Brussels. The flight took one hour and thirty-six minutes.

Senior executives from the Belgian airline, SABENA, who at the time were showing considerable interest, met the aircraft.

The Rotodyne in its chosen environment, approaching
the heliport in the heart of Brussels, en route to Paris,
in 1959.

The Rotodyne then took off from Brussels with six SABENA executives onboard, en-route to Paris, touching down at the Paris Heliport of Issy-les-Moulineux, situated within sight of the Eiffel Tower. The flight took only fifty-eight minutes, and covered 165 miles/265.5km. The same journey using conventional airlines required two hours and fifty-four minutes, and involved two coach journeys to the airliner terminals, which were well outside their respective cities. The Rotodyne carried ballast on all the transit flights to represent the maximum payload.

The Rotodyne flew each day of the flying display at Le Bourget, but also included a visit to the SHAPE headquarters at Versailles, where several VIP flights were made carrying senior NATO officials. The aircraft returned to London from Paris in exactly one hour, covering 180 miles/289.7km.

The company considered the visit to the Paris show and the flight via Brussels to be an undoubted success; a fact that was subsequently supported by the Kaman Helicopter Company expressing an interest in building and marketing the Rotodyne under licence in the United States.

The Bridge-Laying Exercise

A demonstration of the Rotodyne's capability to carry complex underslung loads was undertaken when the aircraft carried a large bridge structure. Believed to be the largest of its kind ever lifted by air anywhere in the world, the bridge measured 10ft/3m by 7ft/2m, with a length of 103ft/31m, almost twice that of Rotodyne itself.

The demonstration was carried out before senior officers and government personnel at Stanlake Park, near White Waltham. The Rotodyne showed that it could lift a cumbersome load vertically, move it at a higher speed than a conventional helicopter, and place it accurately on the ground. This was the first time that Rotodyne had been seen operating in the flying crane role, having so far only been considered purely as a vertical take-off civil airliner for city-centre operations.

Attached by cables to the central point under the fuselage, the bridge section was lifted vertically from the airfield at White Waltham and then transported three miles (5km) to the river. The bridge section was fitted with removable wooden fins to stabilise the load. This exercise was also considered important as a demonstration of the Rotodyne's capability in a military role.

The bridge lifting and positioning exercise. The bridge was almost twice the length of the Rotodyne, and required temporary fins to stabilise it. This demonstration was considered important in order to attract military and commercial interest.

The Rationalisation of the British Aircraft Industry, 1960

Towards the end of the 1950s it was becoming clear that Britain could no longer keep up the high expenditure on defence demanded by the Cold War. In 1957, the Ministry of Defence, led by Duncan Sandys, produced the infamous White Paper, which stated that the role of the manned fighter would be superseded by land-based guided weapons.

This led to the cancellation of a number of projects, and placed the British aircraft industry into a very difficult position.

During this same period the civil market was turning towards America for the next generation of airliners, and orders for British products were not materialising. The result was that most British companies were finding it difficult to stay financially viable. There were in fact too many companies competing for too few orders from a government which was cutting back.

It was made clear from official sources that future orders would be placed with the companies which were prepared to group together to form larger and more efficient organisations.

There were at the time some twenty major aircraft companies in Britain, most of which could trace their roots back to the First World War, if not earlier. During the period 1959 to 1960 there was a trend of regrouping, during which most of the familiar names disappeared.

Company	Grouping, post 1960
Armstrong – Whitworth	
A V Roe	
Blackburn	
De Havilland	Hawker–Siddeley Group
Folland	
Gloster	
Hawker	
Bristol	
English Electric	
Hunting	British Aircraft Corporation
Supermarine	
Vickers	
Beagle (Auster/Miles)	Independent – closed in 1969
Handley-Page	Independent – closed in 1970
Scottish Aviation	Independent – merged with BAe in 1977
Shorts	Independent – joined Bombardier in 1989

When the dust had settled and the various mergers and acquisitions had been finalised, there were only two major aircraft companies in the UK, namely: the British Aircraft Corporation, and the Hawker-Siddeley Group. These two companies eventually joined to become British Aerospace (BAe), in 1977.

The above table shows what happened to most of the major aircraft companies that comprised the British aircraft industry pre-1960. None of this activity included the helicopter industry, which proceeded independently.

The British Helicopter Industry

At the time of the rationalisation there were four companies concerned with the design and manufacture of helicopters in the UK:

1. The Bristol Aircraft Company (Helicopter Division). Bristol had achieved some success under the leadership of helicopter pioneer Raoul Hafner, having brought the Sycamore into production. It was also in the process of developing the Bristol Type 192 Belvedere twin-rotor transport helicopter.
2. The Fairey Aviation Company. The Fairey Company was heavily involved in production of the Gannet aircraft and the FD-2 high-speed delta wing research aircraft. Helicopter activity was almost wholly concerned with the development of the Rotodyne.
3. Saunders-Roe. Saunders-Roe was an aircraft company with a long and distinguished record for the production of flying boats and seaplanes. In the post-war years they extended their activities to include a jet fighter flying boat and missile design, while also working on the massive Princess flying boat and pioneering an entirely new mode of transport, the Hovercraft.

    In 1951 Saunders-Roe acquired the Cierva Helicopter Company, with the intention of diversifying even further into rotorcraft. When the Princess project was cancelled and their proposal for a jet/rocket-assisted fighter was rejected, the company, which was heavily committed to experimental work, went into decline, and finally sold their helicopter and hovercraft interests to Westland Aircraft in 1959. The company was in the process of producing the Skeeter helicopter for the British Army, and the development of a larger turbine-powered helicopter, later to be developed as the P 531, to become the Scout and Wasp for the army and the Royal Navy.
4. Westland Aircraft Ltd. Westland was a long-standing aircraft company, formed in 1915. Based in Yeovil, Somerset, the company had produced a number of fixed wing designs, including the famous Lysander. Throughout the Second World War the factory had been a centre for Spitfire and Seafire production. With the war over, it became necessary to find aircraft work with a peacetime application. In 1946 the Westland board made a policy decision to concentrate all future activity on helicopter design and development. In order to implement this, the company decided to take out a licence to build Sikorsky helicopters.

By 1960 there was a well-established and profitable helicopter business at Yeovil, which produced the WS 51 Dragonfly, the WS 55 Whirlwind, and was in the process of delivering the WS 58 Wessex. As a consequence, Westland now dominated the UK helicopter scene.

The company was also developing their own large twin-turbine helicopter, based on a Sikorsky transmission and rotor which, with an all-up weight of 33,000lb/14,970kg, was a direct competitor to Rotodyne.

It was hardly surprising that Westland, with its strong position, and having already absorbed Saunders-Roe, were able to acquire Bristol and Fairey. By the end of 1960 all UK helicopter interest was under Westland control.

This situation presents an interesting business lesson. Westland, from the outset, had concentrated on producing and selling helicopters, and in the course of ten years had produced over 500 aircraft. The company was well established as a production unit, and had made many lucrative sales in the home market and abroad. Even though Westland helicopters were based on existing Sikorsky designs, each of the adopted aircraft had undergone major re-engineering, and the company had, of necessity, established an effective design and customer service organisation.

The other companies had concentrated on research and development, at considerable expense, and without the support of a strong production base.

Westland acquired the Fairey Aviation Company in February 1960, and with it responsibility for the Rotodyne. Uninformed opinion has often stated that Westland failed

One of the few pictures of the Rotodyne and the Westland Westminster together, seen here at White Waltham, participating in the 1960 Farnborough show. Westland actually abandoned the Westminster project in favour of the Rotodyne. (Photograph courtesy of Maidenhead Heritage Centre)

to pursue Rotodyne with sufficient energy. This could not be further from the truth. Not only was the Fairey design and development organisation kept intact, but Westland actively supported Rotodyne development, at the expense of their own Westminster project, which was finally abandoned and scrapped in September 1960.

In fact the Rotodyne was only engaged on its flight programme for four years and three months, and it is not generally appreciated that Westland were commercially and administratively responsible for the work carried out during the last two years of activity.

Several important tasks were undertaken during Westland's stewardship, such as single-engined run-on landings, underslung loads, flexible pylon assessments, provisional assessments of rotor governing and a noise assessment flight into Battersea.

Much of the design activity for the larger Tyne-powered Rotodyne FA-1 was also undertaken during what might be called the 'Westland years'.

It must be appreciated that the reorganisation had a profound effect on the whole industry, and that it took some time for the new groups to re-establish themselves as viable business organisations.

The Rotodyne hovering at White Waltham in 1961, now declaring Westland ownership and carrying military markings, as apparently it should have done throughout the ministry-financed programme.

The flight into Battersea Heliport went almost unnoticed by the public. As can be seen here, it was indeed a very large aeroplane operating in a very small space.

The Flight into Battersea, March 1961

Such was the concern over Rotodyne noise that it was decided to carry out a flight into Battersea Heliport, situated on the Thames in the heart of London, only 5,000m from the Houses of Parliament. The heliport had, in fact, been built for Westland in 1948, and was operated enthusiastically by the company, who saw it as a visible sign of faith in the future of helicopter operations.

The exercise was given the codename 'Exercise Snowdrop', and was arranged in conjunction with the Ministry of Aviation.

The demonstration took place on 3 March 1961. The Rotodyne made two flights into Battersea, taking off from White Waltham and flying into London along the approved corridor, continuing downriver to the West India Docks, before turning to approach Battersea. Transition and tip-jet light-up took place over the Albert Bridge, and the aircraft descended to the heliport.

On take-off from the helipad, the aircraft climbed vertically to 150ft/40m, and then accelerated, still climbing to pass over Wandsworth Bridge, at approximately 900ft/300m, at which point the tip-jets were cut and the transition completed.

On the first sortie the aircraft hovered close to the helipad without touching down. For the second sortie a normal landing was completed and the aircraft shut down. The all-up weight while operating at the heliport was approximately 33,000lb/24,000kg, and the aircraft was fitted with Type 8c silencers for this exercise.

The helipad dimensions were 125ft x 50ft, or 38m x 15.25m, which, considering the helicopter measured 60ft/18.3m, with a 90ft/27.43m rotor diameter, was a remarkably tight fit.

Seven noise-recording stations were sited around the heliport, with radio contact from the control tower. In addition, thirty individual observers were situated over a wider area (up to 5,000m) to make subjective assessments. Weather conditions were calm and ideally suited for noise recording.

For the second sortie, when an actual landing was made, timing was as follows:

Tip-jets lit – hover	78 seconds
Hover – touch-down	33 seconds
Touch-down – tip-jets OFF	1 second
Total duration	112 seconds

For the take-off and climb-out, timing was as follows:

Tip-jets lit – hover	22 seconds
Take-off – 120ft, vertical climb	30 seconds
Climb-out – tip-jet OFF	89 seconds
Total duration	141 seconds

The peak noise levels measured at the seven recording stations indicated between 101–114 phons.

The thirty observers who were dispersed around the area produced the following results for peak noise levels during landing and take-off:

Deafening	one report	115 phons
Very noisy	five reports	111 phons
Noisy	thirteen reports	103 phons
Moderate	seven reports	97 phons
Low	four reports	96 phons

Recordings were also taken of the aircraft as it flew overhead, at approximately 1,000ft, in the Gyroplane regime (tip-jets OFF). This varied between 94–100 phons, and was classified subjectively as 'low'.

One observer, stationed on Westminster Bridge, stated that he could not measure the aircraft noise levels above that of passing traffic (85–96db).

There was, in fact, no public criticism or complaints concerning aircraft noise arising from either of the two sorties, only two telephone inquiries which were stimulated by curiosity.

As far as the Fairy Aviation Company was concerned, the exercise was a success.

The Rotodyne Order Book

In parallel with the technical programme, the Fairey Sales and Marketing team maintained a strong campaign to establish a market for the Rotodyne, as was evidenced by the establishment of the speed record, the London–Brussels–Paris flight and the aircraft's presence at the Farnborough and Paris shows.

A colourful series of advertisements were placed in the aviation press carrying the slogan 'Look forward to Rotodyne travel'.

A Canadian company, the Okanagan Helicopter Group of Vancouver, placed the first order for a Rotodyne. This was announced at the SBAC Display and Airshow at Farnborough, on 4 September 1958. The order was for a single aircraft with the option to acquire two more.

For the Fairy Aviation Company this event was recognised as a major step forward, including, as it did, North American interest.

Okanagan Helicopters could claim to be one of the largest commercial helicopter operators in the world, flying a fleet of fifty-four helicopters supporting logging activities, oil exploration and geological survey work. With the acquisition of a Rotodyne, Okanagan intended to extend their activity to include passenger services between city-centres in Canada.

The Canadian order was quickly followed by one from Japan Airlines, who required two aircraft with an option for four more, intended for domestic operations in Japan, specifying the larger Tyne powered variant, which was already under consideration as Fairey 'Type Z', and was taking shape as the production version.

In March 1959, New York Airways announced that they had completed negotiations with Fairey Aviation for the supply of five Rotodynes, with an option to acquire a further fifteen, having been granted a licence for the operation of city-centre helicopter services from New York to various towns in the New England states. This important event was accompanied by a statement from the Kaman Aircraft Corporation of Bloomfield, Connecticut, announcing that they had negotiated an agreement with Fairey to become sales and servicing agents for the Rotodyne, which would include a manufacturing licence to produce Rotodyne in the United States. Again, it was emphasised that the NYA order would be for the larger Tyne-powered aircraft. This strong North American interest gave others confidence that Rotodyne had a bright future, having broken into the difficult US market.

Chosen by the world's largest commercial operator of helicopters, Okanagan Helicopters of Vancouver, the Rotodyne vertical take-off airliner will be in service in two to three years' time. The Rotodyne Era of fast, convenient, comfortable travel is closer than most people have realised. Because of its unique potential, the Rotodyne is regarded as an 'airliner of the future'. And so it is. But the threshold of that future is now just a short step away.

FAIREY Rotodyne

Powered by Napier Eland turbo—props

THE FAIREY AVIATION COMPANY LIMITED · HAYES · MIDDLESEX · ENGLAND
and The Fairey Aviation Company of Canada Limited · Eastern Passage · Halifax · Nova Scotia · Canada

'Look forward to Rotodyne travel'; the slogan used on most Rotodyne advertisements, seen here proudly announcing the order by Okanagan Helicopters.

The Rotodyne project was originally intended to provide aircraft for British European Airways, and it was with this in mind that the government had financed the programme.

With confidence based on orders for thirty aircraft, the Fairey Company pursued their negotiations with the government with renewed vigour, with the result that British European Airways declared their intention to acquire six aircraft, with an option for a further six. Following protracted discussions, a type specification for the BEA aircraft (Ref: FA1-BEA-1) was issued, in October 1961, for what was, by then, the Westland Rotodyne. This was also the first occasion that the designation Type FA-1 was used.

As already mentioned, there was also military interest. The Royal Air Force was in the process of laying down a requirement for a medium-sized transport aircraft capable of operation from small unprepared airfields. To this end a version of the Hawker-Siddeley (Avro) 748 Airliner, later to become the Andover, and a short take-off version of the Handley-Page Herald, were under consideration. The RAF, it must be said somewhat reluctantly, agreed to include the Rotodyne for consideration to meet this requirement.

There was also a NATO requirements for a V/STOL medium-range transport aircraft (Ref: AC/170), for which the Fairey/Westland team produced a detailed proposal in November 1961.

The End of the Rotodyne

Following the Battersea exercise, progress was slowed down by engine availability. The Napier Company was already commercially weak. There were few prospects of sales for the Eland so the company's future was reliant upon the success of the Gazelle turbo shaft engine, intended for use in helicopters and, at the time, selected for the Wessex and the Belvedere.

The rationalisation of the aircraft industry also affected the engine manufacturers and, in mid-1961, Napier was taken over by Rolls-Royce, who promptly made it clear that they did not intend to continue support for the Eland. The result was that the turnaround of the development of standard engines for the Rotodyne was slow, which, in turn, had a knock-on effect on the progress of the flight programme.

With the uncertainty brought about by the reorganisation of the airframe manufacturing industry came the prospect that the engine companies were about to be reorganised in a similar fashion. Rolls-Royce stated that they could no longer guarantee delivery dates for the Tyne engine and the New York Airways order and Okanagan Helicopters were tied to specific delivery dates.

Upon completion of the merger with Westland, the government awarded an additional £4 million to fund the Rotodyne development contract and British European Airways declared their intention to purchase six aircraft, conditional upon all the requirements being met, including those regarding noise.

As time progressed, it was becoming clear that the current contractual delivery dates could not be met. It was also evident that development costs would increase, with the result that the cost per aircraft would be higher.

As the selection process for a medium transport aircraft by the Royal Air Force progressed, the service chiefs came down firmly in favour of the Andover, claiming that a short take-off capability was more than adequate for the intended role of the aircraft. British European Airways were faced with the prospect of carrying the development costs alone, coupled with an increase in the cost per aircraft, and there was every indication that the operating costs would be higher still. The result was that BEA withdrew their order.

As a direct consequence New York Airways, Japan Airlines and Okanagan Helicopters also withdrew their interest. A government statement was made to the effect that support for the Rotodyne programme would be withdrawn, although Westland could continue with the programme as a private venture with BEA if they so wished! Official funding for the Rotodyne was finally withdrawn at the end of February 1962.

During a debate on aviation in the House of Commons, on 26 February 1962, the Minister of Aviation, Mr Peter Thorneycroft, made the following statement:

As announced to the House at the time, a contract for the development of the Tyne-engined Rotodyne, to meet military as well as civil requirements, was placed in February, 1960. The Government have been reconsidering the future of the project against the general economic background, and the need to restrict Government expenditure. They have decided that, so far as the military version is concerned, it is necessary to forgo the operational advantages offered by this aircraft in view of the cost involved. At the same time, British European Airways have now informed me that, following a careful reappraisal of their forward plans they have concluded, with reluctance, that the commercial prospects of the Rotodyne on their routes are not sufficiently assured to justify the heavy liabilities involved in the placing of an initial production order. In the absence of any firm production order, Westland has decided that they would no longer be justified in proceeding with the project and steps are being taken to terminate the development contract.

Westland was heavily committed on programmes for Wessex, Whirlwind, Scout, Wasp and Belvedere, and as a company there had never been a culture keen to take on unsupported private ventures. Work on Rotodyne was immediately stopped.

The Rotodyne prototype was government property, and was finally cut up as scrap, in accordance with official instructions, on a symbolically cold day towards the end of 1962. No one has ever actually owned up to responsibility for this act of technological vandalism. A few key parts, namely the rotor head and pylon structure, a small section of fuselage, several tip-jets and a single Eland engine were retained, and for years were on display at the College of Aeronautics, Cranfield, before coming to their final resting place at the Helicopter Museum at Weston-super-Mare. The huge wealth of drawings, reports and technical data has disappeared into obscurity (or anonymous private hands) and little has re-surfaced, in spite of worldwide interest in the technology.

It may be that the decision not to proceed with Rotodyne was correct, on commercial grounds, and that, as a technical advance, it was a case of 'too much too soon'. What is indefensible is the way in which the hardware was destroyed and the design data lost, apparently in accord with official policy. In the half-century that has elapsed since then, no other aircraft or rotorcraft has emerged capable of fulfilling the role of a vertical take-off airliner.

Like the TSR-2, the Rotodyne story represents a lost opportunity; decisions were made in haste, leaving little but time in which to regret at our leisure.

Leading particulars of Rotodyne Type 'Y'

Data drawn from a presented by Dr G.S. Hislop, FRAeS, to a joint meeting of The Royal Aeronautical Society and The Helicopter Society of Great Britain, 7 November 1958.

Rotor Diameter	90ft/27.43m
Rotor Blade Chord	27in/69.0cm
Number of Rotor Blades	Four
Nominal Rotor Solidity	.0637
Rotor Aerofoil Section	NACA 0015
Flapping Hinge offset	2ft/0.6m
Rotor Blade Twist	Zero
Gross Wing Area	475ft²/44,13m²
Wing Span	46.5ft/14.17m
Wing Chord	10.5ft/3.2m
Wing Aspect Ratio	4.5
Wing Section	NACA 23015
Wing Incidence to Fuselage C/L	4° 40ft
Tail plane & Elevator Area (Gross)	163ft²/15.14m²
Tail plane Thickness/Chord	14%
Fin & Rudder Area (Total)	170ft²/15.79m²
Fin & Rudder Thickness/Chord	10%
Tail Unit Aerofoil Sections	NACA Symmetrical
Overall Length of Fuselage	58ft, 8in/17.88m
Overall Height	22ft, 2in/6.75m
Fuselage internal length	46ft/14m
Fuselage internal height	6ft/1.82m
Fuselage internal width	8ft/2.44m
Floor, height off ground	3ft, 5inches/1.04m
Clamshell door size	8ft/2.44m wide x 6ft/1.82m deep
Forward door size	5ft, 10in/1.77m high x 3ft/0.91m wide
Window spacing	36in/0.91m – 10 windows
Track of Undercarriage	24ft, 6in/7.47m
Propellers	Two Rotol four blade – 13ft/3.96m diameter
Gross weight	33,000lb/14,969kg
Disc loading (Hover)	6.14lb/ft² or 29.97kg/m²
Nominal Blade Loading (Hover)	96.4lb/ft² or 470.66kg/m²
Tip Speed (Hover at S/L)	720ft/sec

Power Plant: Two Napier Eland N.E.L.3, turboprops (2,800shp), with auxiliary compressors via a clutch, providing air for four Fairey pressure jet units.

Auxiliary Compressor Mass flow	22.7lb/sec or 10.3kg/sec
Compression ratio at 12,500rpm	4.35/1

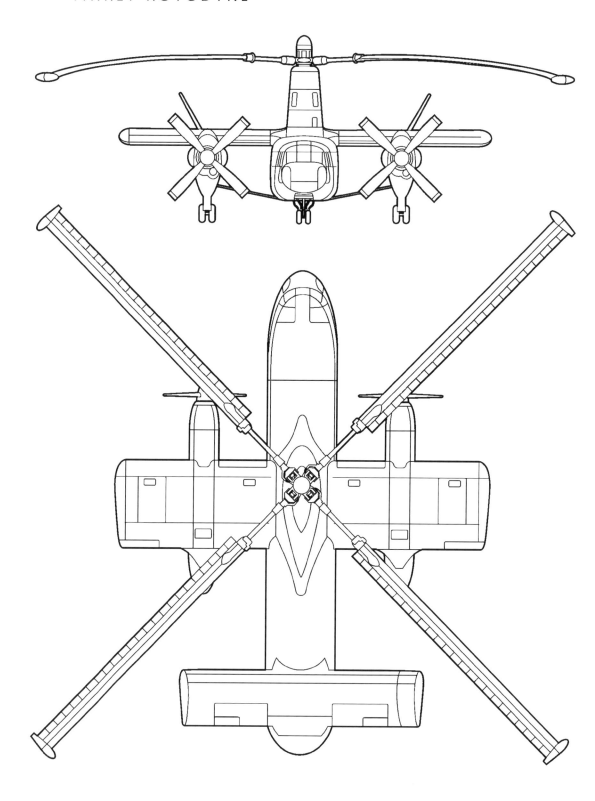

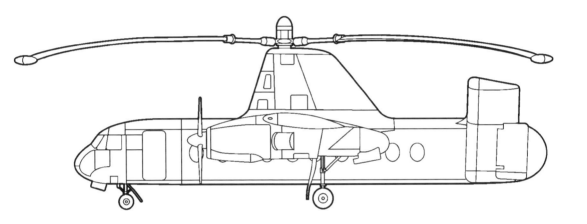

General arrangement of Rotodyne 'Type Y'.

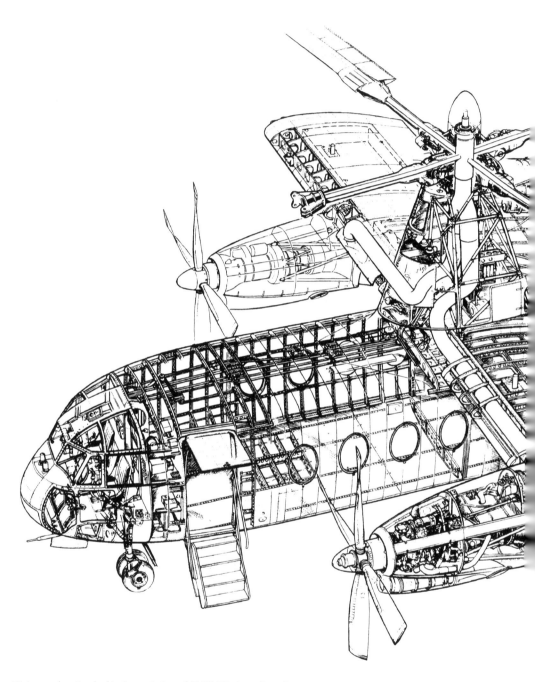

(Cutaway drawing by kind permission of *FLIGHT International*)

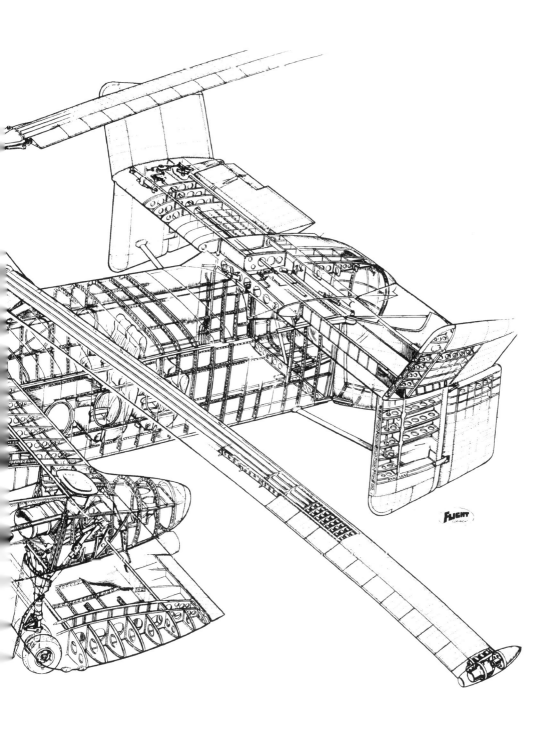

This page: Technological vandalism.

three

THE ROTODYNE THAT MIGHT HAVE BEEN

The Rotodyne was designed to meet a specific requirement for an airliner capable of vertical take-off and direct operation to and from city-centres, with passenger capacity comparable with the equipment in use by the airlines at the time. The prototype Rotodyne was conceived in the belief that, for the foreseeable future, a capability to carry forty passengers would be suitable.

Even this figure had grown considerably by the time the project was launched. It therefore did not come as any surprise that, by the time the prototype had flown, British European Airways were already calling for a larger aircraft to match extended versions of the Viscount and the proposed Vanguard.

Early discussions with potential customers clearly indicated that they too would require a larger aircraft.

The requirements coming from British European Airways and prospective export customers were calling for an aircraft with a capacity for fifty or more passengers, and this would result in a larger aircraft, which in turn would require more power.

The Napier Eland engines installed in the forty-seat development aircraft had only ever delivered 2,560shp. By 1959 the Napier Engine Company was already struggling to survive, and Fairey had no confidence that the development of the Eland to achieve higher power would be successful, or, in fact, that any programme to improve the output of the engine would even proceed at all.

Negotiations were started with Rolls-Royce to consider the installation of the Tyne, which was capable of delivering more than 4,000shp. Proposals for the Tyne-powered Rotodyne soon began to appear, with a larger fuselage, a wingspan of 56ft/17m, and a rotor diameter of 104ft/31.7m, and the all-up weight of the revised aircraft was to be 53,000lb/25,400kg.

At this stage the configuration of the enlarged Rotodyne remained proportionally the same, and would include the installation of a similar auxiliary-compressor arrangement to that already used to provide air for the tip-jets to that used in the prototype.

As time progressed the details of the new aircraft, now known as 'Type Z', began to materialise, showing a wingspan of 75ft/22.9m, a fuselage length of 70ft/21.3m, and a proposed all-up weight of 60,800lb/27,636kg, with a rotor diameter of 109ft/33,2m. It had also been decided that a new stand-alone gas generator, the Rolls-Royce RB176, would be installed to provide air for the tip-jets. The shape and form of the production Rotodyne had been decided.

Towards the end of 1961 specification documents began to appear for both the civil aircraft for British European Airways (BEA) and a military variant for the UK and NATO. The basic construction and configuration of the two aircraft were fundamentally the same, incorporating differences as required to satisfy the respective civil or military roles.

A considerable amount of design and development work had taken place over the preceding two years to establish the size and shape of the new aircraft.

Apart from a dramatic increase in dimension, the basic configuration of the Rotodyne remained the same apart from a noticeable increase in wingspan, also in the case of the civil aircraft the clamshell rear door opening had been abandoned.

Fairey, now part of the Westland Group, re-designated the aircraft 'Type FA-1'. It is perhaps interesting to note that up until this time the production aircraft had been known as 'Type Z', and maybe it was prophetic that Fairey type designations, having started at 'A' and continued alphabetically, reached the end of the alphabet just as the Westland takeover took place.

It was to have been a big aircraft as the following comparison illustrates:

	Military ROTODYNE	CH 47 Chinook
All–up Weight	68.300lb/30,980kg	54,000lb/24,495kg
Cabin Length	47ft/14.3m	30ft/9.1m
Width	9ft/2.8m	7.5ft/2.3m
Height	7ft/2.13m	6.5ft/1.9m

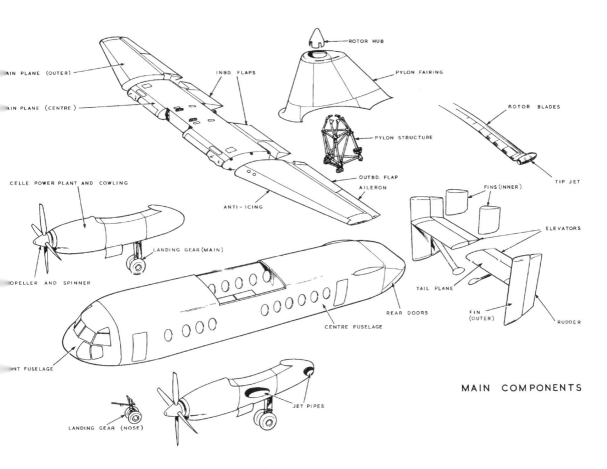

The Rotodyne 'Type Z' (FA-1) military version, showing the main components.

The basic details of the new aircraft were as follows:

Wing Structure

The wing, which had a span of 75ft/22.86m, was to consist of an orthodox box structure with three spar webs manufactured as one item with three major portions; a parallel centre section and two outer tapered sections complete with tips. Main stiff ribs were provided at major stations for flap, fuselage and engine nacelle attachment. In each case assembly was by bolted, replaceable fittings.

Fuel was to be carried in the wings using bag-type tanks, two between the fuselage sides and engine nacelles, and two in each outer section. Between the nacelles and the fuselage, the leading edge was hinged to provide easy access to controls and services. Jacking points were provided at the rear spar between the fuselage and engine nacelles. Flaps and ailerons were of all-metal construction.

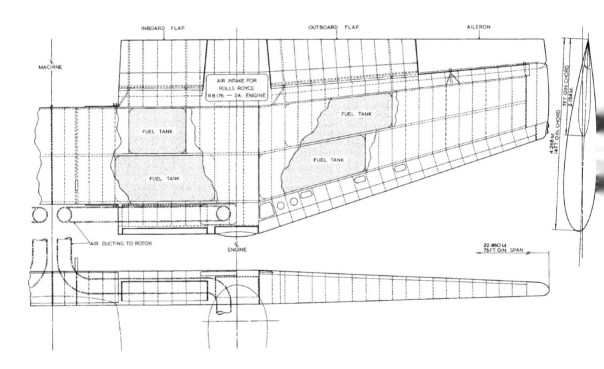

The arrangement of the wing structure, which was substantially larger in area than that of the 'Type Y'.

Fuselage Structure

The fuselage was basically a box of approximately rectangular cross-section, with closely spaced channel frames and intercostal stiffeners, having longerons at cabin roof and floor levels.

The 'box' was closed aft of the pilot's cockpit by the area containing the avionics cabinet, storage facilities, and provision for the main passenger/crew entrance, which took the form of an 'airstair' door on the port side. In the case of the civil aircraft, the rear clamshell doors were dispensed with, and the area contained a baggage hold and toilet facility.

For the military version provision was made for freight and vehicle loading through the rear end of the fuselage, which was split on the horizontal centreline to form two doors, the lower of which was hinged at the bottom to form a ramp, providing an unobstructed entry equal to the dimensions of the fuselage. In order to allow the wing to pass over the top of the fuselage as one continuous structure, a recess was provided in the top of the fuselage, into which the wing fitted, attached to a suitably strengthened fuselage frame.

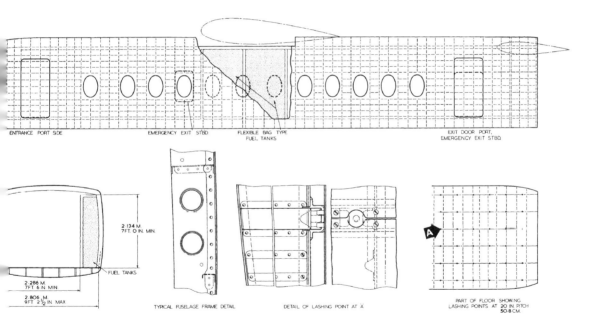

The main fuselage structure maintained the same simple construction techniques adopted for the 'Type Y', to ensure ease of production.

The cabin floor for the civil aircraft comprised of longitudinal beams forming the base for the seat rails to established civil standards.

The military aircraft had an effective floor area of approximately 400ft²/37m², floor attachments were arranged in the standard grid pattern of 20inch/51cm pitch.

Both versions had entrances situated at the rear of the fuselage, on the port side. Additional emergency exits were provided to civil or military standards as applicable. The fuselage windows consisted of vertical ellipses measuring approximately 2.2ft/66cm x 1.5ft/41cm, a total of twelve being installed along both sides of the fuselage at approximately 34in/86cm pitch, the windows being positioned intercostally between longitudinal stiffeners.

Provision for emergency evacuation for both variants met the current British civil requirements.

Tail Structure

The tailplane was mounted on top of the fuselage at the extreme end of the main structure, and was very similar to the arrangement seen on the prototype.

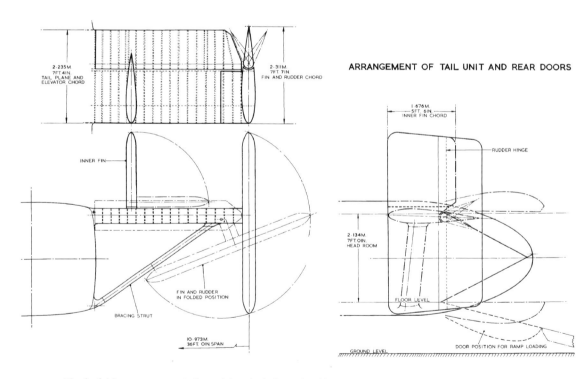

The fin folding arrangement allowed the whole fin and rudder to rotate under the tailplane. The military version included ramp access, which was not standard for the civil variant.

The horizontal stabiliser measured 36ft/11m, and carried full span elevators braced to the bottom of the fuselage. At the tips were the two fin and rudder assemblies. Attached approximately at their horizontal centres, these could be pivoted about their attachment points to retract to a near horizontal position to allow for clearance of the blades when the aircraft was on the ground. There were two additional fins mounted on the top of the stabiliser at a point just outside of the fuselage sides which could be folded hydraulically. The whole tail assembly was of all-metal construction.

Main Rotor Pylon

The rotor pylon was built as an entirely separate unit, and was basically a tubular steel structure transmitting all loads between the airframe and rotor head. The whole structure was housed in a streamlined form, providing a light fairing around the load-carrying structure.

The pylon structure consisted of the tubular steel space frame, pin-jointed to the wing and terminating in a bolted attachment to the rotor head main bearing case. Spring dampers were incorporated in the rear struts to reduce damaging vibratory stresses transmitting from the rotor head to the airframe structure.

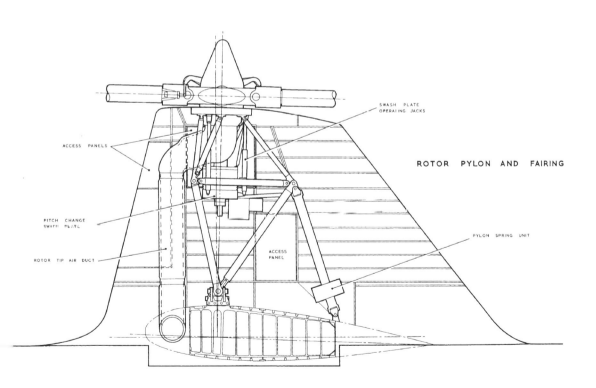

The main rotor pylon was basically unchanged from the configuration developed for the 'Y', and included the spring damper units incorporated into the rear supports.

Rotor Head

The rotor head was of the non-tilting (articulating) type, with collective and cyclic control achieved through a hydraulically operated swash plate. Collective pitch was obtained by raising or lowering, and cyclic pitch by tilting, the swash plate.

Four stub arms, made as an integral part of the hub, carried flapping hinges, drag hinges not being fitted since the flapping angles were small enough to render such hinges unnecessary.

Outboard of the stub arms were four hollow inner spars incorporating feathering hinges and attached at their root ends to the flapping hinges. At their outer ends the spars were grown in size to form the pick-up points for the rotor blades.

The root portion of the head was arranged to allow the air for the jet units to pass through the bore and be distributed equally to the two pairs of tip-jets; the object being to provide two complete air systems, each supplying two blade tip-jets situated as diametrically opposite pairs, thereby ensuring complete separation of the of the twin power systems, providing an efficient arrangement in the event of an engine failure without the need to rely upon shut off valves. A casing carrying two inlet pipes (one from each of the RB176 engines) was mounted below the head, each pipe delivering air to one pair of blades.

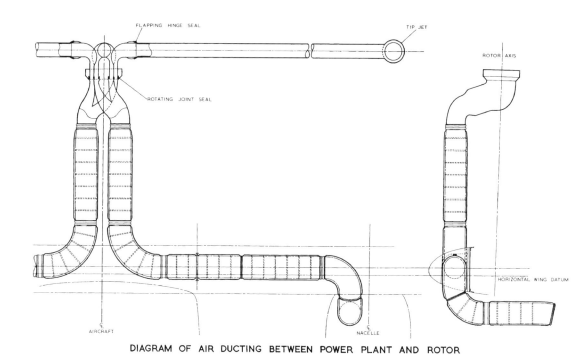

DIAGRAM OF AIR DUCTING BETWEEN POWER PLANT AND ROTOR

The arrangement of air ducting from the RB176 gas generators to the rotor head, supplying air for the tip-jets.

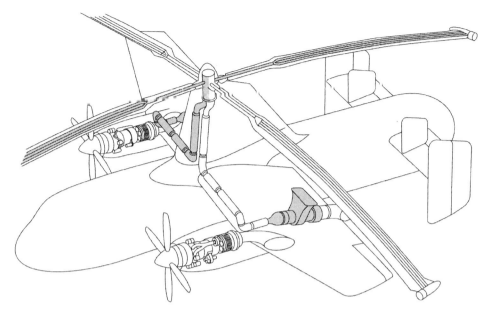

Two Rolls-Royce Tyne engines, and two RB176 gas generators to provide air for the tip-jets, powered the production aircraft. Each RB176 supplied air to diametrically opposite pairs of blades, providing a measure of single-engine capability.

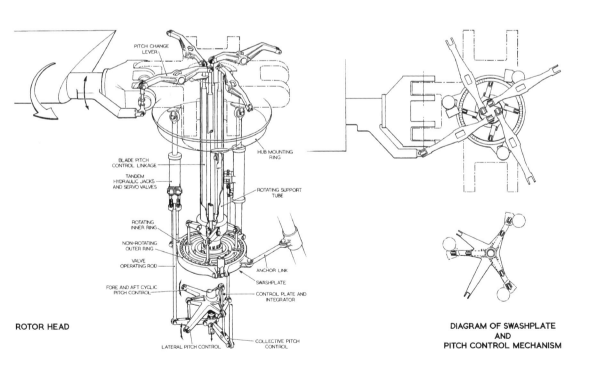

ROTOR HEAD

DIAGRAM OF SWASHPLATE AND PITCH CONTROL MECHANISM

The rotor head control mechanism.

Rotor Blades

Each rotor blade had a main spar of tubular form made of stainless steel. Apart from carrying structural loads, the tube was to act as a duct through which the air to the jet units could pass. A stainless steel nose section was braised to the front of the spar to form the leading edge, while, at the rear, the aerofoil section of the blade was completed by a series of short length, independently mounted, light-alloy boxes attached to lugs braised on to the spar – the boxes being readily detachable for inspection or replacement. The leading edge section carried fuel lines and was surfaced with electrical de-icing mats. The electrical wiring for jet unit ignition passed along the rear of the main spar duct and would be accessible by removal of the trailing edge.

Rotor blade dampers were to be fitted at the inner portion of the blades to reduce oscillating blade stresses and assist with the control of ground resonance.

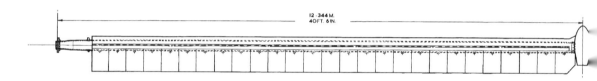

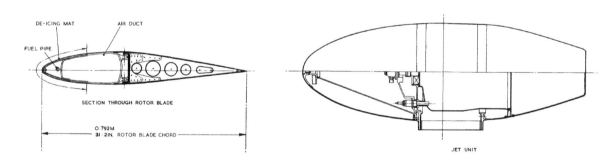

ARRANGEMENT OF ROTOR BLADE AND JET UNIT

The main rotor blade was subjected to a complete redesign. It consisted of a stainless steel main spar, which contained the single steel extrusion duct which carried air to the tip-jets. Electrical de-icing heater mats were also included, representing a new technology in the 1960s.

Cockpit and Controls

The layout of the cockpit and controls did not differ radically from the accepted norm for a helicopter cockpit. The aircraft was designed to be operated by a crew of two, with the captain occupying the right-hand seat, following normal helicopter practice. The central console and roof panels were arranged so as to be fully accessible to either pilot. The main controls were laid out in the accepted fashion for a helicopter cabin, with a central cyclic and a collective pitch lever to the left of each pilot's seat.

In the helicopter flight regime, the controls and their sense of operation followed conventional helicopter usage, with the exception of directional control which was achieved by the differential application of propeller pitch through the mechanism of the rudder pedal circuit. The tip–jet power output was variable over a wide range by operation of the twist grip, situated on the collective pitch control lever, which was to regulate the RB176 output and fuel-to-air ratio. A fully safeguarded trim device was to be provided to regulate propeller pitch in order to keep thrust at a low value.

The full-scale wooden mock-up of the fuselage was assembled at Hayes. The cockpit represented an important feature of this to assess visibility and the layout.

The cockpit was realistically laid out in great detail in the mock-up. The installation included a representation of the state-of-the-art avionics flight instruments, allowing effective cockpit assessment to be undertaken.

This view across the spacious cockpit emphasises a well-laid-out crew station with good external vision.

Flying in the gyroplane regime, operation of the controls remained essentially within conventional usage, engine power being controlled by a throttle lever, and propeller pitch by a propeller control unit functioning within the normal safeguards, such as torque sensitive pitch control, fuel cut-off and oil-pressure failure lock.

The engine HP cock and feathering pump would be operated in turn by the progressive backward movement of the trim lever.

Cockpit dimensions and switch positions were laid out in accordance with contemporary anthropomorphic data.

It is interesting to note that the specifications for both military and civil aircraft include the provision of ashtrays for the pilots, and the comment that 'smoking would be permitted'.

The Main Cabin Area

Freight hold (military)

The main cabin was laid out to a standard typical of any medium-sized military transport aircraft capable of multi-role operations. The available length for stowage of freight was 47ft/4.3m, the fuselage width at floor level was 9.2ft/2.8m and the height was 7ft/2.14m.

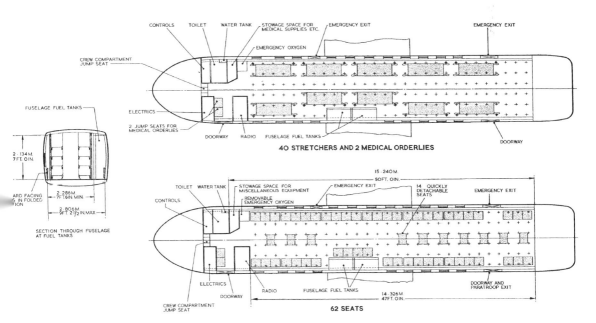

40 STRETCHERS AND 2 MEDICAL ORDERLIES

EQUIPMENT IN FUSELAGE

The cabin included a full set of freight-lashing points, and provision for stretchers or troop seating, to full military transport standards.

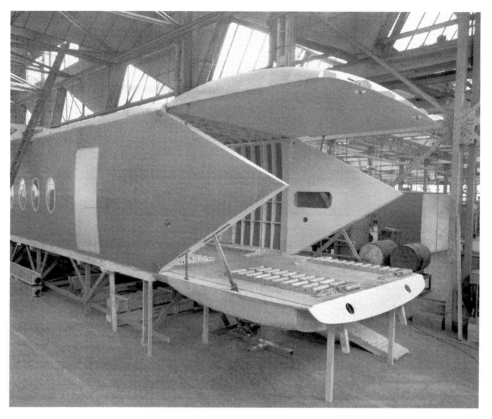

The rear-loading ramp and doors were set out in a 'beaver tail' arrangement, allowing full access for the largest acceptable loads, which often included vehicles.

The freight hold was free of bulkheads throughout the usable area and, to permit maximum flexibility in operation, equipment required for special roles could be quickly and easily installed or removed.

In order to meet the radius of action requirement, the version proposed for NATO included two large integral fuel tanks installed internally on the port side directly under the wing. The additional fuel tanks and support structure created a local reduction in width to 7.5ft/2.28m.

Freight loading would normally be carried out through the large doors at the rear of the fuselage. These contained an integral loading ramp capable of taking any loads that could be accepted by the aircraft. The rear opening cross-section and the angle of the ramp were designed to ensure that no restrictions would be imposed on the loading or unloading of the maximum size loads that could be accommodated. On board equipment included an integral power-operated winch to facilitate loading.

The floor of the freight hold was designed to take high-density loads of at least 200lb/ft^2 or 997kg/m^2. The floor was stressed to accept vehicles with axle loads of 4,000lb/1,815kg.

The rear-loading ramp for the production aircraft gave access to the whole cabin. Ramps were to be standard for military aircraft, and installed on request in civil aircraft.

A 20in/50.8cm tie-down grid of lashing points was positioned so as to provide six longitudinal rows. These lashing points were to be capable of restraining an ultimate load of 10,000lb/4,540kg in any direction. A single row of side lashing points was to be provided at near roof level for securing light loads of up to 1,125lb/510kg.

Soundproofing was to be of the same standard as that provided for the civil aircraft. Provision was be made for the installation of troop seats to carry sixty-two troops and their equipment. Alternatively seat rails could be installed for seating to the civil standard to carry sixty-nine passengers.

Air-conditioning was proposed capable of dealing with temperatures up to 45°C.

An emergency oxygen system was to be permanently installed in the freight hold with suitable connections for use in the casualty role.

In the casualty role provision was also available for forty stretchers or a range of alternative combinations providing for a mixture of stretcher-bound and seated patients. Seating was available for medical orderlies or aircrew as required by their specific roles.

Parachuting was also possible from the rear side door.

Passenger Cabin (Civil)

The civil aircraft was based on the same basic structural shell as the military variant, differing only in the internal layout.

In the late 1950s it was possible to take your car to the Continent by air, and there were a number of companies specialising in this trade. It was with this in mind that provision had to be made for large clamshell doors in the rear fuselage of the Rotodyne.

By the early 1960s it was becoming clear that this cross-Channel trade was not going to be sustainable, and the decision was made not to include rear fuselage loading doors as standard in the civil version. If the facility was required, it would have to be specially ordered and would take the form of that designed for the military variant.

The main cabin had an internal length of 52.25ft/16m, a maximum internal width of 9.75ft/2.95m and a constant height of 7ft/2.13m.

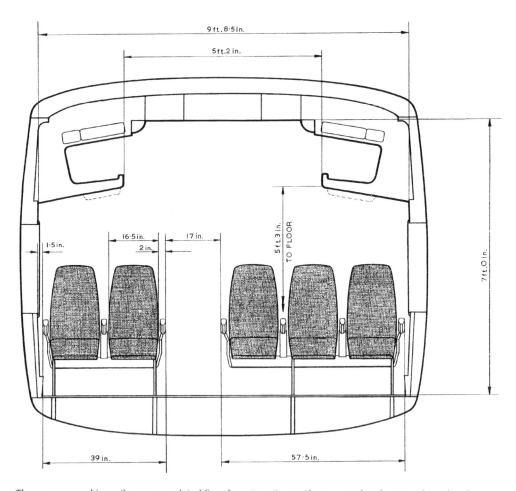

The passenger cabin easily accommodated five abreast seating, with generous headroom and overhead lockers.

The passenger seating laid out in the mock-up for assessment.

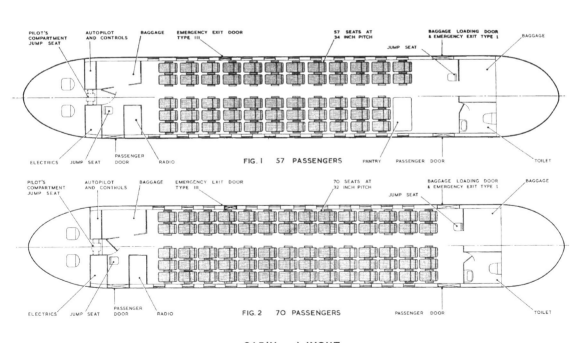

CABIN LAYOUT

The fifty-seven-seat passenger layout, and the alternative high-density seating arrangement.

The standard layout provided for fifty-seven passengers seated five abreast at 34in/0.86m pitch, set out in a two-three arrangement, allowing a gangway width of 17in/0.43m. A high-density layout was also available allowing for seventy passengers at 32in/0.81m pitch.

Provision was made for pantry, baggage stowage and toilet facilities to customers' requirements.

A total of twelve passenger windows, set at 34in/0.86m pitch, allowed for windows to be available for each row of passenger seats.

Passenger entrance doors of the 'airstair' type were situated on the port side at the front and rear of the cabin.

Power Plants

The larger Rotodyne was to be powered by two Rolls-Royce Tyne Mk 562 turbo-prop engines, each with a maximum continuous power rating of 4,955shp. The Tyne was a comparatively new engine originally developed for use in the Vickers Vanguard airliner, which was currently on order for British European Airways. No doubt the use of the Tyne was seen to offer the advantages of using common equipment.

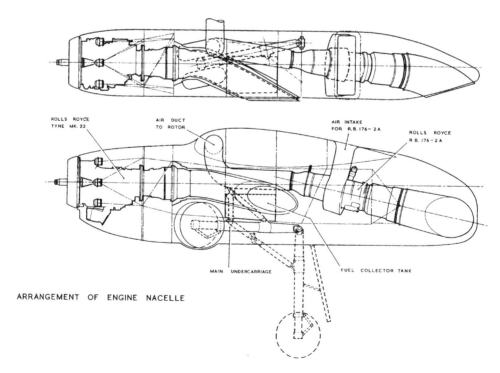

ARRANGEMENT OF ENGINE NACELLE

The engine nacelle arrangement, housing the Rolls-Royce Tyne engine, RB176 gas generator and undercarriage.

A single-stage HP turbine drove the nine-stage HP compressor whilst a three-stage LP turbine drove not only the propeller (via a reduction gear box) but also a six-stage LP compressor. The combustion was cannular.

Protection against icing by the electrical heating of intakes was also provided.

RB 176 Compressors

The supply of compressed air for the tip-jets on the prototype 'Type Y' Rotodyne was provided by an auxiliary-compressor mounted in the Eland engine, controlled by a hydraulic clutch.

For the production aircraft, two separate dedicated stand-alone compressors, designated Rolls-Royce RB176, were selected. The RB176 under development was intended specifically for use in the Rotodyne, and was capable of producing air at a mass flow of 42.9lb per sec/19kg per sec, at a pressure ratio of 6.14:1 at sea level, at 25°C (ISA + 10°C), the maximum contingency rating. They were to be mounted in the engine nacelles aft of the Tyne engines, with air intakes on the upper wing surface and exhausts on the outboard side of the nacelles.

Rotor Tip-Jets

A single pressure-jet unit would be mounted at the extremity of each rotor blade, and was simply a larger version of those used on the prototype.

Each of the RB176 gas generators was arranged to serve one diametrically opposed pair of units in order to minimise the power loss in the event of the failure of one engine. Fuel under pressure would be supplied to the combustion chamber of each unit, the fuel/air ratio being governed by a variable datum automatic regulator. Ignition of the fuel/air mixture would be effected by two high-energy igniter-plugs in each unit, each plug being fed from an independent supply as a precaution against electrical failure.

The tip-jets were to be completely interchangeable, the high-energy igniter-plugs and igniter-boxes being readily accessible, and the combustion chambers replaceable.

Performance

Civil aircraft (Ref: Specification for British European Airways, October 1961).

Power Plants: Two Rolls Royce Tyne 562 turboprops.
                  Two Rolls-Royce RB176 gas generator engines, providing air for four
                  Fairey pressure jets.

Maximum continuous power rating: 4,455shp
One hour power rating: 4,955shp
Aircraft operating weight with fifty–seven passengers: 60,800lb/27,580kg

The specification called for the following guaranteed performance:

- The aircraft had to be capable of carrying a 10,830lb/4,912kg payload, plus one hour's worth of standoff fuel over a stage distance of 200 nautical miles/370km.
- Fuel tankage had to be adequate for a stage of 250 nautical miles/463km, operating in a 40 knots headwind.
- Cruising speed had to be guaranteed at no less than 175 knots or 325km/hr, with a mean cruise weight, at an altitude of 5,000ft/1524m.
- The cruise speed had to be increased to 200 knots or 370km/hr.
- The rate of climb at sea level, with zero forward speed, at take-off weight, with both RB176 engines operating at intermediate power, was to exceed 600ft/min.
- The hover ceiling at take-off weight, with both RB176 engines operating at intermediate power, had to exceed 5,000ft/1524m.
- At maximum take-off weight the aircraft had to be able to hover with its wheels clear of the ground, with one RB176 inoperative and the remaining RB176 running at its maximum contingency rating.

Military aircraft (Ref: Specification for NATO AC/170, 21 November 1961).

Power Plants: Two Rolls-Royce Tyne Mk 22 (Stage 4) turboprops,
                  Two Rolls-Royce RB 176 gas generator engines, providing air for four
                  Fairey pressure jets.

Maximum continuous power rating: 5,725shp
Intermediate contingency power rating: 6,330shp
Aircraft take–off weight: 68,300lb/30,980kg

This specification called for the following guaranteed performance:

- **TAKE-OFF AND LANDING**: Accepting that the Rotodyne is designed for vertical take-off and landing, with full safety in the event of a critical engine failure at any point, the space limitations were not defined by the all-out performance, but purely by the probability area required by the aircraft landing after an engine failure. The space stipulated was a nominal city-centre site measuring 200ft/60m by 400ft/120m. This at maximum take-off weight of 68,300lb/3,000kg at sea level, up to ISA+15°C.
  Note: This also applied to the civil aircraft.
- **SINGLE-ENGINE EN-ROUTE CEILING** (ISA conditions): The ceiling at maximum local weight (start of outward leg) to be 11,000ft/3,355m.

- **OPERATIONAL CEILING** (ISA conditions): The operational ceiling at maximum local weight to be over 20,000ft/6,100m.
- **CRUISING SPEED** (Economic, all engines): 200 knots or 370km/hr (TAS).
- **CRUISE** (ISA conditions): A cruising profile envisaged in accordance with this specification was to accelerate after take-off and accelerate after transition to 200 knots, and to climb at this speed to 15,000ft/4,500m, if the total stage length was over 200 miles. The last 100 miles to the forward base was to be completed below 1,500ft/450m.
- **RADIUS OF ACTION** (With military load at maximum all-up weight): 500nm/927km.
- **FERRY RANGE** (ISA conditions): At the normal maximum take-off weight a ferry requirement of 1,500 miles/2,414km should be met.

Ice Protection Systems

It was planned that both civil and military versions would incorporate protection against severe icing in all regimes of flight down to –35°C.

Wing and tail surfaces were to be protected by an electrical heater element on the leading edges of the wing, tailplane and fins, sandwiched between layers of insulation.

The leading edges would be divided into a number of cyclic areas and breaker strips, the power for these areas being controlled by cyclic switches supplied by alternators.

Electrical heating systems were to be provided for windscreens, propellers and air intakes.

A fluid de-icing system was specified for the rotor blades. As an alternative, an electrical de-icing system was under development, involving the use of heater elements sandwiched between layers of insulation, power being supplied cyclically.

It would be interesting to speculate concerning the level of ice protection proposed for the Rotodyne. In the 1960s few if any helicopters had clearance to fly in icing conditions. Indeed, the whole process of rotor icing was not fully understood and it was only twenty years later that serious flight research into ice accretion and its removal was undertaken with any commitment. Several current helicopters now incorporate blade de-icing systems, but even as they enter service, the finer points of the icing clearance are the subject of debate.

The introduction of heated rotor blades was well ahead of the game at the time, and it is one area where the introduction of Rotodyne into service may have brought about a significant advance in capability for all helicopters some twenty years earlier.

Radio and Navigation Equipment Fit

Viewed by modern standards the radio and navigation fit could not be considered complex, but the proposed installations reflected the highest standard available at the time.

Civil aircraft

VHF communications up
VOR/ILS localiser
Glide slope indicator
Marker
ADF
Decca Mk 8 with a large-scale flight log
Crew/Cabin staff equipment
Cabin address system

Military aircraft

UHF/VHF communications radio
Collins 618 T or Marconi AD 460 HF radio
UHF or VHF emergency standby
Crew intercom
IFF Mk 10 transponder
Blue Orchid Doppler radar
UHF Homer (ARI 18120)
Rebecca Mk4

Design and Development Activity

By mid-1959, when the first orders were placed by Okanagan Helicopters and New York Airways, it had become clear that the demand would be for the larger aircraft, which was already under consideration for British European Airways.

It was estimated that a further £8–10 million would be required in order to undertake the work, of which the government promised to contribute half, including support from official establishments and test facilities such as RAE Farnborough.

By the time Westland had acquired the Fairey Aviation Company, work was already in progress on the design of the bigger Rotodyne, now known as 'Type Z'. The configuration, structural detail and selection of systems and equipment were well in hand.

Development testing had started in a number of critical areas, and work had commenced on the assembly of a full-scale mock-up at Hayes.

Production planning, including negotiations for the procurement of equipment and materials, had been initiated, and some work had started on the manufacture of detailed items. The first airframe had been allocated a constructors build number (9430), and a military serial number (XH249). Such was the confidence that the programme would proceed.

Full-Scale Mock-Up

A representation of the fuselage of the new aircraft was assembled in the assembly shop at Hayes. It must have been an impressive sight, measuring 70ft/21.3m in length, with a full cockpit layout and representative rear-loading doors.

Built of wood, with a marine ply skinning, the mock-up was used extensively by designers and draughtsmen to confirm the positioning of items of equipment and to assess the ergonomics involved in their operation. The representative cockpit layout was seen to be of particular value. Assessments carried out in the facility included both civil and military applications.

Tip-Jet Units

As early as 1960 work was started to adapt the rig facility at White Waltham to accept the new larger jet unit, a prototype of which had been manufactured and delivered to White Waltham for testing.

Discussions were started with Rolls-Royce to determine how best to adapt the Rolls-Royce Avon installation to provide sufficient mass flow of air to run the new units.

Initial tests were primarily concerned with shakedown and assessment of instrumentation and rig facilities, and to obtain some early impressions of the flow patterns within the unit's combustion chamber.

Tests began on the large pressure-jet unit for the 'Type Z' in 1961, seen here installed in the test cell at White Waltham.

Noise

Noise suppression was probably seen as the biggest single obstacle for which a solution had to be found. A large twelve-lobe silencer, similar to the 'Type 8c' units, used with some success on the 'Y', had already been designed, and representations were to be seen on wind tunnel models.

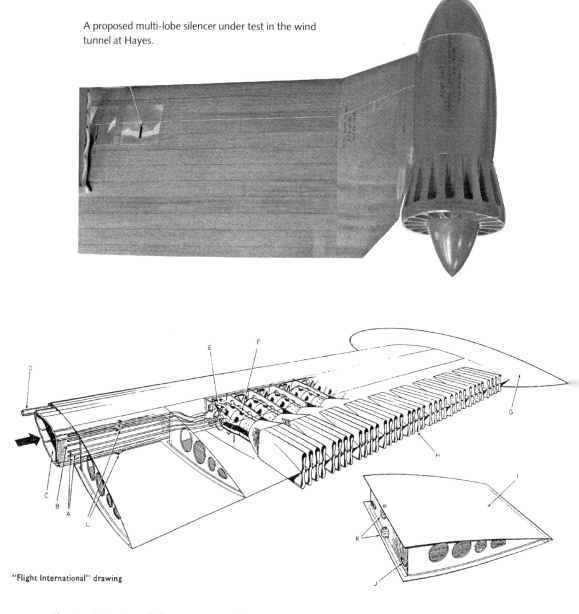

A proposed multi-lobe silencer under test in the wind tunnel at Hayes.

"Flight International" drawing

The nine-jet tip-jet and silencer system, which promised a significant reduction in noise levels.

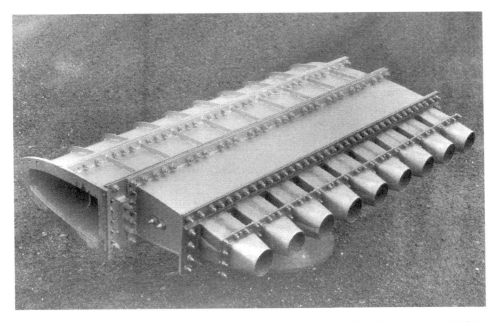

A prototype of the proposed system had already been constructed and tested on the spinning rig at White Waltham.

Extensive tests were undertaken on the noise rig at White Waltham, which indicated that a noise reduction of as much as 16db might be achievable.

Tests had already been carried out on a small ('Type Y' sized) nine-jet unit with considerable success. The unit consisted of nine separate small units, each with its own combustion chamber arranged in a row on the trailing edge at the blade tip. It was a very complex arrangement, and the process to provide air evenly to each of the nine small combustion chambers would have presented a developmental challenge.

The system had been tested in the static running chambers, and had even been run without burning on the spinning rig.

A basic silencer presenting a slotted double H pattern had been fitted to each of the nine units and tested against standard circular orifices on the static noise rig.

The indications were that a noise attenuation of approximately 16db could be achieved, and that this would be enough to satisfy the British European Airways criterion.

Test Models

A 1:9 scale model of the complete aircraft was produced to commence wind tunnel testing to assess drag. This was the largest that could be accepted in the Hayes tunnel. A considerable amount of testing had taken place by the time all work on the Rotodyne project was stopped.

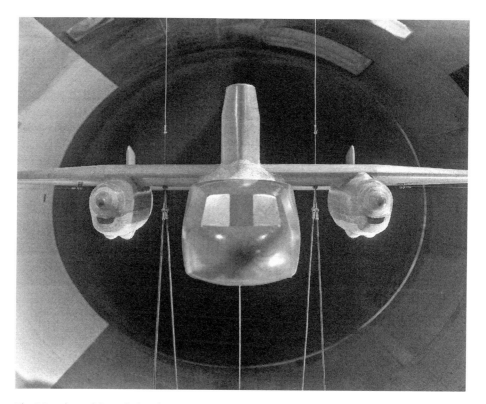

The 1:9 scale model installed in the wind tunnel at Hayes.

Because of the additional wingspan of the 'Z' (FA-1) Rotodyne, the 1:9 scale model was the largest that could be accommodated.

A large accurate model was produced to determine the optimum position for radio and radar aerials.

A dynamic model with fully representative airframe stiffness and mass was constructed to assess vibration and dynamic characteristics.

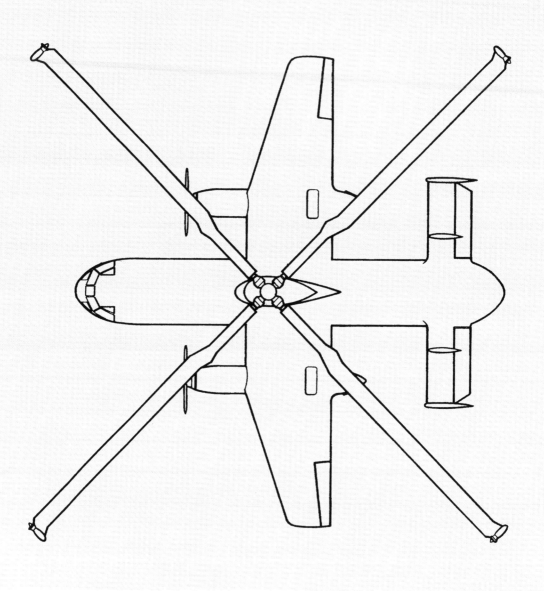

The Hayes model shop had also produced a large fully representative model for aerial placement tests.

A dynamic model fully representative of structural stiffness and mass was also constructed to assess vibration in advance of full-scale testing.

It can be seen from the nature of the above tests and facilities that the design of the production aircraft was well in advance, and there was every confidence that the flight programme could be brought to a satisfactory conclusion.

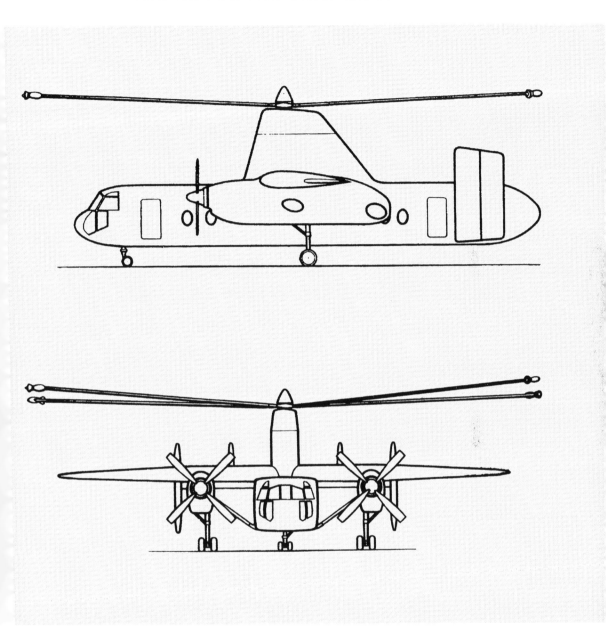

General arrangement drawing.

Leading particulars of Rotodyne 'Type Z' (FA–1)

Data drawn from the type specifications of the Westland Rotodyne for British European Airways (issued October 1961):

Rotor Diameter.	109ft/33.223m.
Rotor Blade Chord.	31.2in/0.792m
Number of Rotor Blades	Four
Nominal Rotor Solidity	.0608
Rotor Aerofoil Section	NACA 63–215 (modified)
Flapping Hinge offset	1ft, 8in/0.508m
Rotor Blade Twist	Zero
Gross Wing Area	898ft²/83.427m²
Wing Span	75ft/22.86m
Wing Chord (centre section)	14ft/4.267m
Wing Chord (tip)	7ft/2.134m
Wing Aspect Ratio	6.25
Wing Section (centre)	NACA 23018
Wing section (tip)	NACA 23012
Wing Incidence to Fuselage	C/L 2°
Tail plane & Elevator Area (gross)	264ft²/24.526m²
Fin Area (each outboard)	107ft²/9.941m²
Fin Area (each central)	32ft²/2.973m²
Rudder Area aft of hinge (each)	38.6ft²/3.586m²
Tail Unit Aerofoil Sections	NACA 0014
Overall Length of Fuselage	70ft, 6in/21.488m
Overall Height	27ft, 3in/8.306m
Fuselage internal length	52ft, 3in/15.926m
Fuselage internal height	7ft/2.134m
Fuselage internal width	9ft, 8.5in/2.959m
Floor, height off ground	4ft/1.219m
Forward door size	5ft, 10in x 2ft, 9in/1.778m x 0,838m
Window size	2ft, 6in x 18in/0.762m x 0.457m.
Track of Undercarriage	25ft, 4in/7.772m
Propellers	Two DH four blade – 15ft diameter/4.572m
Gross weight	60,800lb/27,578kg.
Disc loading (hover)	6.5lb/ft² or 31.735kg/m²
Nominal Blade Loading (hover)	107lb/ft² or 522.4kg/m²
Tip Speed (hover at S/L)	720ft/sec or 219.45m/sec

Power Plant: Two Rolls-Royce Tyne 562 propeller turbines (4,955shp)
Two Rolls-Royce RB176 gas generators
Mass flow 43.9lb/sec or 19.912kg/sec
Compression ratio 6.14/1

four

FIFTY YEARS ON

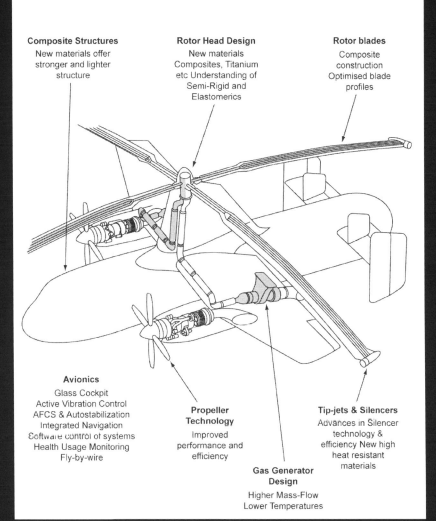

Composite Structures
New materials offer
stronger and lighter
structure

Rotor Head Design
New materials
Composites, Titanium
etc Understanding of
Semi-Rigid and
Elastomerics

Rotor blades
Composite
construction
Optimised blade
profiles

Avionics
Glass Cockpit
Active Vibration Control
AFCS & Autostabilization
Integrated Navigation
Software control of systems
Health Usage Monitoring
Fly-by-wire

**Propeller
Technology**
Improved
performance and
efficiency

**Gas Generator
Design**
Higher Mass-Flow
Lower Temperatures

Tip-jets & Silencers
Advances in Silencer
technology &
efficiency New high
heat resistant
materials

THE ROTODYNE
FIFTY YEARS ON

Over half a century has gone by since the Rotodyne first flew, and during the years that have elapsed there have been no serious attempts to re-visit the technology, and proposals to take compound helicopters to a level where they could be considered for service have rarely advanced far beyond the experimental stage.

The materials and processes used in the construction of aircraft in the mid-1950s were still basically the same as those used for aircraft production during the Second World War. The term 'Avionics' was a word yet to be coined to describe airborne electronic equipment, and these were generally confined to radio and radar, although helicopter autopilots were under development.

While the Rotodyne was undergoing its flight-testing, the Soviet and the US space programmes were unfolding, and in the wake of all this activity technology has advanced at an unprecedented pace.

The use and availability of air transport has also continued to grow year by year, to the point where the available airspace can no longer meet the demand. The availability of airfield space is already becoming a problem, and the air traffic control facilities necessary to maintain the safe and efficient movement of air transport are stretched to the limit.

The use of VTOL has frequently been proposed as a means of alleviating runway congestion and complex air-traffic networks which the short-haul provincial airlines generate.

This was indeed one of the objectives of tilt rotor programmes such as the civil V-22 and Eurofar, neither of which have progressed beyond the project stage.

Military requirements and expectations have also advanced, demanding performance and capability well beyond that achievable with conventional helicopters, and this has brought the convertiplane to the fore as a possible solution. The V-22 Osprey programme is a prime example. The V-22 dates back to 1982, or even further if one includes proof of concept work carried out with the XV-15, which was built to demonstrate technological capabilities. The V-22 Osprey is now in service, but the costs escalated far beyond the original estimates and the programme has taken twenty-five years to come to fruition. Nevertheless, it represents the only large convertiplane technology programme with any production prospects, and has deeply committed the two major companies concerned. It has also consumed a high proportion of US government defence expenditure.

These comments should not be construed as criticism of what has evolved to become a very fine aircraft, but it does indicate the level of commitment necessary to launch projects intended to bring about any substantial advance in capability, and the debate as to whether such convertiplanes can be developed into larger aircraft continues.

A compound helicopter such as the Rotodyne does offer an alternative approach. It is, therefore, worth considering what would be different if a new generation Rotodyne were proposed to meet the needs of the twenty-first century.

The whole process involved in designing, testing, manufacturing and certifying new aircraft has been subject to change as technology has progressed. In most cases there is every indication that the advances could offer solutions to some of the areas that presented problems forty years ago. But it must be appreciated that in many cases new areas of uncertainty would almost definitely arise, presenting the engineers with a whole new range of difficult choices.

Reliable and properly substantiated composite structures are now commonplace in all areas of airframe manufacture. The noise of the rivet gun and the litter associated with fabricated metal has almost disappeared from the factory floor.

Airframes are now manufactured and assembled in surgically clean conditions, with strict tool control.

Computer-Aided Design and Computer-Aided Manufacturing (CAD/CAM) have also brought about an equally dramatic change in the drawing office and machine shop, and the calculating power available to the technician has resulted in the ability to predict and substantiate component lives to even greater accuracy for all materials.

The use of composites for airframe manufacture has resulted in lighter, stronger structures, coupled with the ability to consistently achieve aerodynamically clean profiles.

The introduction of **Composites** has had a particularly dramatic effect on rotor blade design. The ability to manufacture complex profiles with such accuracy has resulted in a considerable improvement in blade performance.

Westland took full advantage of all the features available from the use of composites to design the BERP (British Experimental Rotor Programme) **Blades**, with which they took the world speed record in 1986, achieving 249.1mph/400.87kph. However, most composite materials are severely affected by heat. The air passing through the blade from the gas generator has a temperature of 150–200°C, far higher than that which can be tolerated, and this is a good example of a new problem arising from the use of new materials.

Rotor Head design has advanced. Semi-rigid rotors are now a practical proposition and materials such as titanium are more readily available.

Gas Generators and **Turbo-Props** have improved in efficiency and are capable of producing a higher mass flow of air, such that it is possible for the tip-jets to operate at lower temperatures. It may even be possible to consider cold cycle operations.

Propeller technology has advanced, offering improved performance and efficiency.

The physics of **Noise** generation and suppression are much more clearly understood and, coupled with the advances in materials, should result in improved silencer performance and durability at high temperatures.

The nine-jet unit, which was only given a preliminary assessment at the end of the Rotodyne programme, promised a substantial reduction in noise levels, and can now be subjected to a full programme of testing to hopefully fulfil its promise.

The field of technology that has seen the most spectacular rate of progress over the last fifty years has to be that of **Avionics**, affecting every area of the aircraft's operational capability.

Glass cockpits are now the norm, offering an economy of layout, the whole flight instrument display being reduced to as few as six displays, all of which have a built-in redundancy to safeguard against failures. Biggles would hardly recognise his cockpit in this day and age!

Health Usage Monitoring Systems (HUMS) record temperature, pressure, vibration, stress and flight parameters throughout the time that the aircraft is operating. The recordings can be downloaded for trouble-shooting and maintenance records. From this information component lives can be accurately assessed and often extended, and potential failures exposed.

Navigation and Communications equipment represents another area that has witnessed significant advances. The accuracy achievable with Global Positioning Systems (GPS), backed up by inertial systems, make it possible to position an aircraft to the level of accuracy demanded by the tasks in hand. Such systems can be integrated into **Automatic Flight Control Systems (AFCS)** which, in turn, can fly the aircraft automatically through the approach and touch-down sequence.

Automatic Flight Control Systems coupled with rotor governing and auto-stabilization, all of which were new areas of development for helicopters when the original Rotodyne was undergoing its test programme, now make it possible to operate the aircraft automatically throughout its flight profile, reducing pilot workload with increased safety.

Active Vibration Control not only offers the prospect of a smooth ride but also reduces the perceived vibration levels in the cabin and equipment bays, with the result that component lives could be extended.

The probability is that a new generation Rotodyne would incorporate **fly-by-wire** controls. A flight control system that would use electronic wiring, instead of mechanical or hydraulic linkages, to control the actuators for the conventional control surfaces and/ or rotor controls.

Challenging Factors

Advanced technology may well provide solutions to many of the problem areas that were experienced during the original Rotodyne programme, but it has to be appreciated that new technology will bring with it new problems requiring resolution.

It also follows that the challenge may not only arise from technical issues but from the management of the programme and the operation of the aircraft.

Noise was always perceived as one of the primary reasons for the Rotodyne's demise. The use of tip-jets would almost certainly bring this to the fore as a major problem that would have to be solved. Subjective opinion was consistent in stating that the Rotodyne was excessively noisy, even when operated with fitted silencers, and it was generally agreed that the 'chuff chuff chuff' noise that came over in certain phases of the aircraft flight was perceived as particularly oppressive.

The AgustaWestland AW-101, with BERP IV blades. Advances in composite materials and construction techniques have made it possible to perfect the aerodynamic shape and mass of the blades to achieve optimum performance.

The quantitative measurements taken at the time demonstrated that it was possible to meet the noise criteria laid down by British European Airways and the certifying authorities, and there was confidence that further improvement would be achieved with the new silencer systems under development, but it cannot be assumed that this will be accepted by the environmental lobby of today, and local airfield residents will always be hard to please.

Proponents of VTOL and STOL airliners frequently argue that the use of such aircraft requiring only short runways (if any) would lead to a reduction in the size of airfields. Unfortunately, the large long-haul airliner is likely to remain with us for some considerable time. Even if shorter runways were achievable, the space taken up for the operational infrastructure such as air traffic control, passenger terminals, security services, freight handling, baggage control, etc., cover such an area, that any advantage would be minimal. Most passengers would also expect to use the same check-in and boarding facilities for their flight transfer, a situation that is not easily achievable.

The use of electronic displays have revolutionised cockpit design. The displays can be reconfigured by the pilot for the appropriate phase of the flight, and the system includes multiple redundancy to safeguard against electrical failure.

The integration of rotorcraft into the air traffic control system is already proving to be a difficult problem. There have already been numerous attempts to establish the comparatively simple process of operating city-centre to airport shuttle services using helicopters, most of which have encountered difficulties and, at best, operate under sufferance.

It is quite common practice for helicopters to be forced to taxi long distances to the dispersal point, for fear of Foreign Object Debris (FOD) generated by rotor downwash.

The issues involved in the operation of VTOL aircraft, whether fixed-wing or rotorcraft, in all weather, using the same airways pattern and approach paths, in parallel with existing airways traffic, has yet to be addressed.

The public perception of rotorcraft is that they are less safe than fixed-wing craft.

Even forty years on the technology involved is still cutting edge. Any development programme will have to be managed with great care. The complexity of programme management has increased in recent years and, all too frequently, the need to meet programme milestones is in conflict with the prudence required to ensure safety and minimise risk. All this has a tendency to result in escalating costs.

The design, development and production of such an aircraft would extend the resources of the largest of corporations, presenting considerable commercial risk. It would be desirable to ensure that there was a civil and military interest even though this would further complicate the process of achieving certification and service release.

International collaboration would help increase the field of interest in the project, although this in itself can further complicate management and cost issues.

five

RENAISSANCE

During the half a century that has elapsed since the demise of the Rotodyne, conventional helicopters have progressed, gaining, as might be expected, from the technical advances that have affected all forms of aviation.

Helicopters are in regular use throughout the world, operating in the heavy lift role at weights and performance comparable with that originally envisaged for the larger Rotodyne.

There is, however, a demand for even greater capacity and performance, which may only be achievable by the convertiplane or compound helicopter. It is in this area that the technology developed for the Rotodyne may yet come into its own.

There has always been a considerable amount of interest in Rotodyne in the United States. Charles Kaman frequently stated that it was an act of folly to abandon the project when success was imminent.

The withdrawal of government support, which in turn led to the decision by Westland not to continue as a private venture, can probably be justified; however, the destruction of the prototype, and the way in which the data was allowed to be dispersed without trace, can only be described as technological vandalism. Nobody has ever admitted responsibility for this.

With the need for improved capability beyond that achievable by conventional helicopters, there has followed renewed interest in compound helicopters and the use of autorotation to achieve the required higher performance.

There are at least two groups in the United States currently working on projects that draw upon the technology demonstrated by the Rotodyne:

Carter Aviation Technologies (Carter)

Research and development of a new and unique gyroplane design began in 1992 when Jay Carter Jr conceived of a way to redesign the conventional rotor system. His goal was to decrease rotor drag by slowing the rotor down in flight while maintaining rotor control, achieving a high rotor tip speed ratio (exceeding $\mu=1$), thereby opening the way to higher forward speeds. The Carter gyroplane incorporates a high-efficiency autorotative rotor system, off-loaded by a wing. The concept has become known as Slowed Rotor/ Compound (SR/C) aircraft technology. Carter's use of a wing to off-load the rotor in autorotation has a relationship to Rotodyne.

The small, dedicated Carter team constructed their first prototype, the CarterCopter Technology Demonstrator (CCTD), as a test platform and technology demonstrator, and began flight testing in 1998. The CCTD incorporated composite construction, a high aspect ratio wing with a span of 32ft/9.75m, a Carter-designed 8ft-diameter high-efficiency propeller and a 34ft/10.36m-diameter high-energy rotor system. The five-place development vehicle had a gross vertical take-off weight of 4,500lb/2,041kg. On 17 June 2005, during a test flight for the US Army, the CCTD achieved a tip speed ratio of $\mu=1.02$ at a forward speed of 173mph/278.4kph – the first rotorcraft in history to advance past $\mu=1$.

The CarterCopter Technology Demonstrator (CCTD), which, in the course of its test programme, successfully demonstrated that flight was achievable with a rotor operating at μ=1.

With the success of their first prototype, Carter is currently in the process of building a second gyroplane incorporating refinements learned through seven years of extensive testing procedures and covered by more than seventeen patents. The second-generation aircraft is a four-place Personal Air Vehicle (PAV) that was designed through a NASA Award. The new aircraft is being developed for commercialisation as both a civilian and military airframe. The PAV's 45ft/13.72m rotor and wingspan will provide greater VTOL and flight efficiency. The use of a twin turbocharged 350hp engine will provide maximum speeds of 242mph/389.4kph. Gross vertical take-off weight is 3,000lb/1,360.8kg with a 1,000lb/453.6kg useful load. Range is projected to be close to 800 miles/1,287km at 12,500ft/365.8m AMSL.

A significant aspect of Carter's technology is that it is scalable, and the company has completed preliminary design studies for two VTOL transports, the CH and the CHT.

The Carter Heliplane (CH)

The scalability of Carter's technology allows it to be incorporated into a variety of aircraft sized for specific workloads and environments. The Carter Heliplane, CH-45, is sized to perform small-scale transport for civilian and military purposes such as search-and-rescue. With a 45ft/13.72m wingspan and rotor diameter, the CH-45 will have the ability to access small clearing areas, and yet will be able to carry a significant 2,000lb/907kg

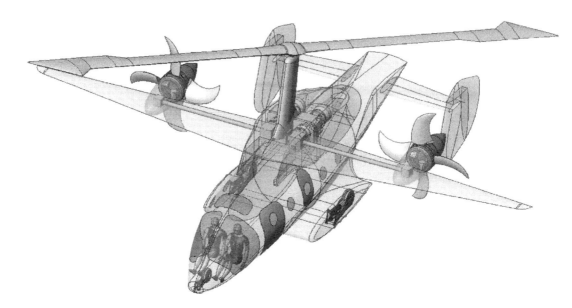

The Carter CH-45 proposal for a high-speed search and rescue heliplane which could take off as a helicopter and, once in flight, be de-clutched and the rotor allowed to autorotate.

load, in addition to its fuel. The CH-45 will have a minimum cruise speed of 400mph/ 644kph, and a range of 1,150 miles/1,850km. In addition, it will also have true hover and sling-load capabilities. The current concept is for the aircraft to use two turbine engines mounted in the fuselage, connected through drive shafts and gearboxes to the rotor and the wing-mounted propellers. Varying pitch on the propellers will provide the anti-torque needed for hovering flight, similar to a tail rotor on a helicopter. A clutch will be used to disengage the rotor to allow it to autorotate during high-speed cruises.

The Carter Heliplane Transport (CHT)

The largest of Carter's designs is the CHT-150. The aim with the CHT is to produce a heavy-lift VTOL transport exceeding the payload and flight performance of the C-130 Hercules, and able to carry 200 commercial passengers or 220 military troops. The US Army has recognised the CHT as a possible candidate for their proposed air-manoeuvre transport programme.

The CHT will be a gyroplane like the CCTD, but like the CH it will include the pilot option to take-off, hover and land like a conventional helicopter, with its rotor in direct drive, using its twin pusher propellers to counteract torque by the application of differential pitch. In forward flight it will convert to a gyroplane, offloading the rotor by means of its high-aspect ratio, high-efficiency wing. Carter stipulates that during

The Carter CHT-150 transport heliplane proposal, offering a large military transporter comparable to the C-130 Hercules, with the capability for STOL or VTOL operation.

this process rotor speed will be reduced to minimise profile drag and maximise flight efficiency, applying the technology demonstrated with the CCTD.

The scale of the CHT is impressive:

Wing span:	150ft/45.72m
Fuselage length:	106ft/32.31m
Rotor diameter:	150ft/45.72m
Propeller diameter:	24ft/7.32m
Max gross weight:	330,000lb/149,690kg (VTOL mode)

The CHT will be designed to cruise at 208mph/333kph at mean sea level; the fuselage will be pressurised to operate at 40,000ft/9,906m. At 32,500ft/9,906m MSL, its cruise speed at best L/D should exceed 400mph/644kph.

Groen Brothers Aviation

Groen Brothers Aviation Inc. (GBA) is a company dedicated to the design and production of gyroplanes. The main activity over the past sixteen years has been devoted to the design and development of the Hawk 4 four-seat gyroplane, which holds the distinction of being the world's first turbine-powered gyroplane.

With the development, certification and production planning for the Hawk 4 well in hand, GBA have turned their attention to convertiplane technology, and have expressed an interest in the development of commercial Gyrodyne platforms, using the features established with the Rotodyne.

Part of the GBA philosophy is the concept that existing fixed-wing airframes can be adapted to accept rotor systems, and to this end they have successfully modified and flown a Cessna 337 Skymaster airframe to accept a Hawk 4 rotor system, powered by a single propeller turbine, to operate as a gyroplane to demonstrate the viability.

The next phase of the programme would be to produce a larger demonstrator vehicle by adapting an Antonev An-28 airframe (nineteen-seat commuter) under the name GBA Gyroliner. The Gyroliner would incorporate all the features of the Rotodyne, including a tip-jet drive for the rotor. It must be appreciated that the Gyroliner is simply a project study, and an ITP (Intention to Proceed) has not been declared.

The GBA Heavy Lift Gyrodyne

As a direct progression of their interest in gyroplane technology, in 2002 Groen Brothers Aviation Inc. responded to a perceived requirement for a heavy lift rotorcraft for military service. To this end they started work on a study for a heavy lift Gyrodyne.

The Hawk 4, turbine-powered gyroplane established the Groen Brothers as a rotorcraft company, and set a new standard for gyroplanes in general aviation.

The GBA proposal set out to adapt the C-130 airframe to accept a tip-jet drive rotor system, but the design of a purpose-built airframe of similar dimensions was also a consideration.

The GBA Heavy Lift Gyrodyne (HLG) would be, in every sense, a 'new generation Rotodyne', operating in a similar fashion, but taking full advantage of the technical advances that have evolved in the fifty years that have elapsed since the original Rotodyne programme.

The HLG proposal allowed for a four turboprop 'Hercules look-alike' arrangement, but an alternative version powered by two large turbofans was also offered.

The arrangements to provide air for the tip-jets were subject to review.

It has been fully appreciated by GBA that it is not a question of simply 'cobbling together' a heavy lift rotorcraft from a C-130 airframe. The programme would call for new airframes, modified at the build stage to accept helicopter dynamic forces, and might, in fact, require a purpose-designed structure.

The advantage to be gained by using an existing airframe structure comes from the fact that the planning, procurement and tooling process would, to a large extent, already be in place, keeping production costs to a minimum.

The GBA heavy lift gyroplane proposal offered a large military transport with VTOL capability, using the C-130 Hercules airframe.

The dimensions of the HLG are as follows:

Wing span: 100ft/30.48m
Fuselage length: 110ft/33.53m
Rotor diameter: 112ft/34.14m
Max all-up weight: 132,000lb/59,874kg

Heliplane

In November 2005, the US Defense Advanced Research Projects Agency (DARPA) selected a GBA-led team to design a proof of concept high-speed, long-range, vertical take-off and landing (VTOL) aircraft for use in combat search and rescue roles.

This modern rotorcraft, which draws heavily upon Rotodyne technology, named the 'Heliplane' by DARPA, could well be the next generation rotorcraft, meeting economy and performance goals not considered achievable by any other type of VTOL aircraft.

GBA's contract, a $6.4 million award to develop the preliminary design and perform key technology demonstrations, represents phase one of the potential multiyear $40 million four phase programme. The Heliplane is designed to exploit GBA's Gyrodyne technology, offering the VTOL capability of a helicopter, the high-speed forward flight of an aeroplane, and the safety, simplicity and reliability of a gyroplane.

Early in 2008, GBA and DARPA completed a system requirements review of the rotor, leaving only one remaining milestone to be met in the first phase of the project.

The Heliplane team includes: Groen Brothers Aviation, Georgia Tech, Williams International and a highly renowned team of aerospace consultants. Negotiations are in hand with Scaled Composites of Mojave to undertake the finalization of the airframe design.

On the government team, under DARPA, the Heliplane team receives important support from NASA Ames and the army's AFDD team at NASA Ames Research Centre, in addition to leading rotorcraft technologists who, for decades, led much of the US advanced rotorcraft development efforts.

The GBA/DARPA Heliplane project for a high-speed search and rescue rotorcraft is currently ongoing, and if brought to fruition will truly be a 'new generation Rotodyne'.

Appendix 1
The Pilot's Viewpoint

The leading test pilot throughout the Rotodyne programme was W.R. (Ron) Gellatly. He and his co-pilot, John Morton, flew the aircraft throughout its entire development, and their personal contribution has to be considered among the programme's greatest assets.

In August 1962 the magazine *Flight* published an article by Ron Gellatly entitled: 'Rotodyne Pilot's Viewpoint'. Although the article repeats many of the points already made in the preceding chapters of this book, it is considered that the statement reflects the professionalism of the Fairey engineering team, and summarises much of what was achieved:

In its last three years of flying, the experimental 'Rotodyne Y' obviously suffered from political indecision. This bedeviled all aspects of the project, but, apart from making target dates impossible, programme continuity was kept and all the major test areas except one had been covered when the contract was cancelled. The notes describe broadly some of the handling work and results procured during the 455 sorties flown on the prototype.

After the early success of the transitional flying technique had been established (the changeover from helicopter to aeroplane flight, and back again), this unusual manoeuvre was considered satisfactory, and no substantial drill changes were made thereafter. In all, 302 transitions were made each way, virtually without incident, and the inherent handling safety and simplicity of these manoeuvres was considered well proven.

Early in 1959 it was thought expedient to establish an official speed record. The 100km closed-circuit course was selected as that most representative of the cruise ability of the aircraft, and the Class B.2 record for convertiplanes was taken at 307.22km/hr, in January 1959.

This record stood until October 1961, when the Russian, Kamov, exceeded it by 28.78km/hr. During practise and actual runs for the record we collected a great deal of information which had to be gained anyway.

Control and Stability

Whereas the original design had been based on a 130 knot cruise, we found that the 'Y' had an economic cruise capability of around 150 knots. In consequence, at this speed, the wing was tending to do too much work, and stick positions were getting too far aft, with rotor flapping, stress levels and vibration also becoming too great. Rectification meant changing the whole wing/rotor relationship by reducing the wing incidence from about 4° to 0°. This brought the mean longitudinal stick positions in cruise to around zero cyclic, and a minimum flapping condition, at the same time, permitted much greater control margins for high-speed manoeuvres.

Lateral control was entirely cyclic, and this became progressively less effective with forward speed as rotor rpm was progressively reduced. Coincidentally, the sloping upper fins, with their dihedral effect, introduced a cross-coupling in lateral/directional control which was quite unacceptable. The first modification here was to make the upper fins vertical, which cured the worst of the rolling tendency with yaw. In the wing-incidence change, ailerons were fitted and linked directly to the lateral-cyclic control at all times, and the combined effect of these, with the vertical fins, gave normal aeroplane rolling control and response in the cruise regime, together with an absolute minimum increase in rotor flapping during the most violent rolling manoeuvres. Later, to overcome some low-angle, low-frequency, directional oscillations of about 2° each way, a third upper fin was added and yaw stability characteristics were then considered adequate for the full manual case, without auto-stabilization. Work in this area was vital to the seventy-passenger version, since the configuration of that aircraft was irrevocably similar to the prototype, and therefore suffered from the same short tail-arm, and limited fin aspect-ratio to meet the rotor droop and flapping cases. In the final design for the production aircraft, four upper fins were incorporated.

A major development task was to prove the engine-out asymmetric-thrust cases and the associated control in yaw. Helicopter asymmetric flight was easily and adequately checked. The half-powered rotor was, in itself, symmetric in thrust, and even with low-thrust main engines (some 25 per cent down on brochure power) an adequate power margin was available for missed landings and overshot cases.

In autogiro single-engine flight handling was much the same as in the other twin-engine machines in this condition, accepting that control of rotor speed intro-duced an additional feature and demanded large elevator angles to trim with speed in the glide.

Early on we realised that the 'Y' control scheme (where the elevator was the main selector of fuselage attitude, and hence wing lift, and the longitudinal cyclic was the main manoeuvre control), although perfectly adequate for test work, would be unsatisfactory in service. The separated functions of rotor and airframe trim introduced a second pitching control, which needed a new technique in manoeuvre. Consequently, much of the performance and the autogiro handling tests were directed at designing a control scheme for the cruise regime which would be, in essence, akin to a standard fixed-wing machine. Our solution was to link the elevator to the longitudinal cyclic (with an overriding elevator trim) for both flight states, and to disconnect longitudinal cyclic from the stick in the cruise regime, when the rotor was to be under the control of a duplicated governor. Before the limits of governing cyclic and elevator-range could be settled we flew numerous trim tests to establish the parameters. Our biggest problem in getting this information was finding dead-calm air for accurate answers, at the desired pressure altitudes, and this seldom prevailed for any prolonged period over England.

Trim results were fed into the design of the rotor governor, which on the prototype was a single system with rather complicated safeguards, which on the production aircraft was to be a fully duplicated system for both flight regimes. Helicopter governing was achieved through the auxiliary-compressor intakes controlling power to the rotor. In autogiro governing came from small displacements of longitudinal cyclic, and the effects of this in pitch were to be countered by the autostabiliser, through the elevator. Sperry undertook development of the governor and, after a series of proof runs on the full-scale rig at Boscombe Down, the single experimental system was fitted and flown successfully through complete helicopter sorties. The final job for 'Type Y' was to prove autogiro rotor governing, with controls modified to the production aircraft scheme as described, and this was scheduled to commence just as support was withdrawn from the project.

'Type Y' was designed to fly at 33,500lb/15,876kg max at take-off. In the normal course of development we took the rotor to an overload maximum of 38,000lb/17,237kg, and this was used to cover the external load-carrying role, which had not initially been intended for this particular machine. Naturally at high overload the rotor was beginning to reach limits in some conditions, and this showed up in the flare to hover. External load carrying in temperatures up to 27°C included high-bulk, low-density loads such as the MEXE Bridge, and high-density, small-bulk loads of up to 8,050lb/3651kg. No handling problems were met throughout these tests, apart from the loss of rotor efficiency in the flare.

Throughout the flying programme the longitudinal centre of gravity was opened up to a range of 18in/46cm, and included the full-speed and manoeuvre envelope at these limits.

Vibration

The alleviation of vibration was a continuous job, which took us through a host of tests, some with applied modifications and some for gathering data only. In early flying the cockpit suffered from severe tray resonance in the classic helicopter vibration conditions, but by the end of development all fourth-rotor (which was the only frequency of note) had been eliminated, and the only complaint we pilots could make was of a propeller-frequency buzz on the instrumentation boom.

In the final vibration-modified state, lag-plane dampers had been fixed to the blade 'lamp post' stub arms, fin-weights and tailplane damper-struts were fitted, and a flexible pylon structure installed, and in this condition the vibration standard in the passenger cabin was brought to within the BEA comfort criteria. All vibration reduction was achieved with no stiffness modifications to the main fuselage, and the design information gained for a tuned structure was enough to guarantee a low vibration level on the production aircraft.

Noise

Much ill-informed criticism was leveled at the subjective noise at take-off and landing with tips lit. The attenuation programme had in fact reduced this down to 96db by the time the development contract was cancelled. A point which most critics failed to appreciate was that the tips lit time in service was only going to approximate one minute at take-off and at landing and, with the flight profiles evolved, low-frequency subjective noise levels for such short periods would have been unlikely to cause annoyance.

The flight paths for safety and minimum noise nuisance were to be a vertical climb at take-off to 250ft/76,2m, before accelerating in forward flight through a point 600ft/182.9m above the heliport, 600ft/182.9m from the pad, and a standard approach angle of 15° for landing. Further large benefits in noise attenuation were envisaged to come from proper heliport design. To prove some of these points, with this underpowered, partially-attenuated prototype, we made two flights over London and into the Battersea Heliport, on a dead calm morning, and no complaints were raised.

The Achievement

Numerous demonstrations were made in both military and civil roles, and these were used to work on operating flight techniques and to settle operators' design requirements. In particular, instrument flying, without autostabilization, was most satisfactory, and we often demonstrated transitions from helicopter to autogiro and back again in cloud, at less than 500ft/152m above the ground. Over 800 passengers, including a fair proportion of the world's airline chiefs, service chiefs, and British MPs, were flown as a demonstration of the inherent safety of this prototype vehicle of radical design, and to emphasise our (and others') faith in the configuration.

'Rotodyne Y' demonstrated conclusively that a large economic transport VTOL was a practical proposition for today, not for fifteen years' time, and that the unloaded rotor and tip drive meant a tremendous breakthrough in performance and handling, in comparison to pure helicopters and other forms of convertiplane.

It is true that some pure helicopters, under carefully controlled conditions of weight, and in very steady flight states, with very restricted component lives and with virtually no maneuver margin have, for short periods, attained speeds equivalent to the Rotodyne; but no other VTOL has yet flown to compare with the public demonstrations made year after year where, with up to thirty-five souls aboard, this experimental aircraft was flown-by at 175kts/325kph, and pulled into a steep climbing 'g' turn with no adverse handling effects.

This is only one of many measures of the achievement of the Rotodyne, and one reason why we should immediately and confidently face a larger and faster design for an operational aircraft.

August 1962

Appendix 2
A Picture of Rotodyne

For its first flight, the prototype was left with its natural metal finish, carrying only the serial number XE521, in black, on its fins.

As trials progressed, markings were added; the pylon was painted white with a blue logo and title, and the name Fairey Rotodyne was placed on the fuselage, in blue. The serial number, XE521, was now also painted blue.

By 1958 a full set of civil-style markings, in blue, had been applied, complete with a generous display of the Fairey logo. The military serial number was retained.

The Rotodyne was repainted prior to the London–Brussels–Paris flight in 1959, retaining the same basic blue and white colour scheme, with the Fairey logo removed.

The Rotodyne as it appeared for the Battersea landings in 1961, now sporting a third fin.

The 'Westland' Rotodyne prior to Farnborough 1961, proclaiming its ownership loudly and clearly for all to see, and carrying national markings as it should have done from the very beginning.

The Rotodyne was remarkably manoeuvrable, seen here breaking left after an air-to-air photographic session. (Photograph by kind permission of *FLIGHT International*)

The shape of the vertical take-off airliner as envisaged 'fifty years too soon'. The compact shape of the Rotodyne is shown to advantage in this photograph taken from above. (Photograph by kind permission of *FLIGHT International*)

Opposite: The Rotodyne on the approach for landing at the Hayes factory, in July 1959, for the installation of passenger seating in preparation for the SBAC show at Farnborough.

Left: The aeroplane-like lines of the Rotodyne are clearly displayed in this view, which also emphasises the size of the rotor. (Photograph by kind permission of *The Aeroplane*).

The Rotodyne at work, picking up the 110ft bridge element.

A very big aeroplane on a very small helipad. The Rotodyne shortly after landing at Battersea in 1961.

Above right: An early demonstration of loading vehicles through the 'clamshell' rear doors to meet the requirements of the car-ferry role.

The Rotodyne in its element, flying over the Thames at Greenwich and Dockland.

Lifting off from White Waltham in 1958.

Wherever it went the Rotodyne attracted attention, as seen here at the Alee Verte Heliport, in the centre of Brussels, surrounded by senior officials from the Belgian national airline SABENA. (Photograph by kind permission of SABENA)

The Rotodyne made several appearances at the Farnborough Air Show, seen here on static display in 1959. (Photograph by kind permission of Fred Ballam)

An early demonstration of the 'clamshell' rear doors, which allowed access to the full width of the cabin for larger items of freight or vehicles.

References

No individual volume has yet been produced which is dedicated to the Rotodyne project. It does, however, receive coverage in several books, magazine articles and technical papers, all of which serve to provide data on a project which has retained interest over half a century, and whose hour may yet come again.

Charnov, Bruce H., *From Autogyro to Gyroplane: The Amazing Survival of an Aviation Technology* (Preager, 2003)

Coates, Steve, *Helicopters of the Third Reich* (Classic)

Taylor, H A., *Fairey aircraft since 1915* (Putnam, 1974)

Wood, Derek, *Project Cancelled: The Disaster of Britain's Abandoned Aircraft Projects* (Janes, 1986)

Relevant Technical Papers

British patent 673870, *Improvements Relating to Rotorcraft* (J.A.J. Bennett & A.G., Forsyth, September 1949)

Dipl Ing A., Stepan, *Jet Propulsion of Rotor Blades* (The Helicopter Association of Great Britain, October 1949)

V.A.B. Rogers, *Problems Associated with the Strength Assessment of Rotor Blades* (The Helicopter Association of Great Britain, April 1957)

Dr G.S. Hislop, *The Fairey Rotodyne* (Helicopter Association of Great Britain & The Royal Aeronautical Society, November 1957)

Dipl Ing A. Stepan, *The Pressure Jet Helicopter* (The Royal Aeronautical Society, February 1958)

K.T. McKenzie, *Aerodynamics Aspects of the Fairey Rotodyne* (The Royal Aeronautical Society. December 1959)

Articles

Several articles have been produced at various times featuring the Rotodyne, some more technically accurate than others. The following list represents the best examples of good technical journalism:

FLIGHT International, 9 August 1957. (Fairey's Big Convertiplane Nears Completion: a Detailed Description.)

The AEROPLANE, 15 November 1957. (Fairey's Vertical Take-off Transport.)

AERONAUTICS, August 1958. (The Self-sufficient Vehicle.)

FLIGHT International, 9 August 1962. (Requiem for the Rotodyne: An account of Unusual Problems Met and Solved.)

The Fairey Film Unit

Fairey were heavily involved in the design and development of guided weapons. An important part of this work included the filming of firing sequences. When development started on the Fireflash air-to-air guided weapon it became clear that the filming of airborne firings would require a professional touch.

A small film unit was formed at Heston with the primary function of filming the airborne firings as an essential part of the technical record.

The film unit personnel, who had been drawn from the film industry, flew in the chase aircraft to obtain records of every event.

The unit was soon in demand throughout the company to film other test activities and produce publicity films.

The films produced to publicise Rotodyne were of a very high quality, and should be included in this section as a valuable technical reference. Copies are rare and access difficult, but a short edited sequence is viewable at www.youtube.com

The Colour of the Rotodyne

The Rotodyne carried the same basic colour scheme throughout the programme, comprising only of blue and white, with the main parts of the airframe left in their natural metal finish. Some definition of the shade of blue used is of interest to modellers, and with this in mind some effort has been made to determine the precise colour.

A small panel with the fragment of the blue writing remaining survived the destruction of the aircraft, and this was assessed by a paint specialist and subjected to a 'pantone' comparison, which resulted in a 'pantone' reference: **2746**.

It must be noted that time may have affected the shade a little, but without any specification reference, and coming from the original aircraft as it did, the above definition is probably the best available.

It should also be remembered that the 2746 shade refers to the aircraft as it was at the end of the programme. The aircraft underwent a full repaint at mid-programme, and although the basic colour scheme remained the same, it cannot be certain that the same shade of blue was used for the original finish.

Index

Visit our website and discover thousands of other History Press books. **www.thehistorypress.co.uk**

Printed in Poland
by Amazon Fulfillment
Poland Sp. z o.o., Wrocław